Jennifer

AMISH LADIES'
COOKBOOK

....FOR AMISH LADIES WITH

OLD HUSBANDS

HEARTS 'N TUMMIES COOKBOOK COMPANY
A Dinky Division of Quixote Press
3544 Blakslee St.
Wever, IA 52658
1-800-571-2665

INDEX

APPETIZERS

CRAB MEAT PIE

8 oz. pkg. cream cheese   ½ small bottle catsup
1 can Alaskan crab meat   4 tsp. horseradish

Split cream cheese in half for ease in smoothing in a 11x7-inch dish. Crumble crab meat over the cheese and then spread on catsup and horseradish (mixed). Spread on crackers and munch.

SHRIMP DIP

1 can (6½ oz.) de-veined shrimp   ¼ C. cocktail sauce
1 (8 oz.) & 1 (3 oz.) pkg. softened   ¼ C. Miracle Whip
  cream cheese

Whip cream cheese, cocktail sauce, and Miracle Whip in bowl till smooth. Drain shrimp and stir in mixture with spoon until it's mixed, but not too fine. Spread on finger sandwiches or use as a dip for vegies or chips.

LITTLE MEAT BALLS

2 lbs. ground pork
2 eggs

1 env. onion soup (dry)
Crackers

Mix all ingredients, shape into small round balls and brown.

EASY SAUSAGE APPETIZERS

2 lbs. seasoned ground sausage
5 C. Bisquick

20 oz. grated Cheddar cheese

Mix together and form into flattened 1½-inch round patties. Bake on ungreased cookie sheet at 350° for 15 minutes. May need to bake longer if sausage is not browned.

CROUTONS

3 (12 oz. ea.) pkgs. oyster
  crackers
2 env. Hidden Valley Ranch
  dressing mix

1 tsp. garlic powder
1 tsp. dill weed

Shake together in large brown grocery sack. Drizzle 1 C. oil over and shake well. Store in sealed containers.

COOL-AS-A-CUCUMBER DIP

2 large cucumbers
2 T. cider vinegar
2 T. garlic salt
1 env. (1¼ oz.) sour cream
  sauce mix

1 (8 oz.) pkg. cream cheese
  (softened)
¼ tsp. sugar
Hot pepper sauce, to taste

Peel, seed, and chop cucumbers to size of corn kernels. Combine with vinegar and garlic salt; refrigerate overnight. Just before serving prepare sauce mix according to package directions. Thoroughly press liquid out of cucumbers to prevent dip from becoming too thin. Blend cucumbers with cream cheese and stir in prepared sour cream sauce mix, sugar, and hot pepper sauce, to taste. Serve chilled with vegetables, crackers or chips. Makes 3 cups.

VEGETABLE PIZZA

2 (8 oz. ea.) pkgs. Pillsbury
  Crescent dinner rolls
2 (8 oz. ea.) pkgs. cream cheese
  (softened)

⅔ C. mayonnaise
1 tsp. dill seed (optional)
¼ tsp. onion salt
¼ tsp. garlic powder

Spread rolls out on ungreased 11x15-inch cookie sheet and bake at 400°
for 10 minutes (golden brown). Cool. Cream together rest of ingredients and
spread over crust. Sprinkle assortment of your favorite grated raw vegetables
over pizza — cucumber, radish, celery, tomato, carrots, etc.

TUNA PATE

1 (8 oz.) pkg. cream cheese
2 tsp. chili sauce
2 tsp. oregano

1 tsp. minced onion
1 T. Worcestershire sauce
1 small can tuna

Mix all together and use as a cracker dip.

CHEESE BALLS

4 (3 oz. ea.) pkgs. cream cheese (softened)
6 oz. Blue cheese (softened)
6 oz. processed Cheddar cheese spread
2 T. grated onion
1 C. ground pecans (½ for mixture & ½ for topping)
½ C. finely chopped parsley or parsley flakes (½ for mixture & ½ for topping)
1 tsp. Worcestershire sauce

Mix until all is well blended and shape into a ball. Wrap in waxed paper then in foil. Refrigerate overnight. One hour before serving, roll cheese ball in ½ C. nuts and parsley. Serve with assorted crackers.

TUNA DIP

1 C. dairy sour cream
¼ C. grated Parmesan cheese
1 (3½ oz.) can tuna (drained & flaked)
1 hard-cooked egg (chopped)
1 T. lemon juice
1 tsp. dry Italian salad dressing mix
Paprika

VEGETABLE DIPPERS:
Carrot sticks
Celery sticks
Red pepper rings
Cauliflower
Green onions
Turnip slices
Radishes
Zucchini

In a small bowl, combine first five ingredients and garnish with paprika. Chill and serve with vegetable dippers.

CHEESE AND HAM APPETIZERS

3 oz. pkg. cream cheese (cubed)
5-6 large stuffed green olives
2 T. mayonnaise

½ tsp. prepared mustard
4 thin slices cold boiled ham

Put first 4 ingredients in blender. Blend until smooth. Spread this mixture 1/8-inch thick on ham slices; roll each slice as for jelly roll. Wrap in waxed paper or foil. Chill an hour or two then slice in ¼-inch slices. Place slices on small crackers to serve.

CRACKER SPREAD

2-3 oz. pkgs. cream cheese
1 (4 oz.) pkg. dried beef

3 little green onions
Dash of Worcestershire sauce

Mix together and spread on crackers. This is thick so it makes a good spread but too thick for a dip.

FRUIT DIP

3 oz. cream cheese
½ C. powdered sugar
2 T. milk

¾-1 tsp. cinnamon
¾ tsp. nutmeg

Beat well and add 8 oz. Cool Whip. Serve with almost any fruit. Oranges, apples, grapes, and pineapple are especially good.

BREADS

'Tater Pancakes

2 eggs
½ small onion
1 tsp. salt

2 T. all-purpose flour
¼ tsp. baking powder
3 C. cubed raw potatoes

Put eggs, onion, salt, flour, baking powder, and ½ C. potato cubes in blender. Cover and process at ''grate'' until potates have gone through the blades. Add remaining potatoes, cover and process at ''chop'' only until all potato cubes have passed through processing blades. Do not over blend. Pour onto a hot well-greased griddle.

"Right Now" Raisin Bread

2 C. raisins
2 tsp. baking soda
1½ C. boiling water
1 C. sugar
¼ C. shortening

1 egg
1 tsp. vanilla
2¾ C. all-purpose flour
1 tsp. baking powder
½ C. black walnuts

Sprinkle soda over the raisins and pour boiling water over them; let stand ½ day or overnight. Cream shortening and sugar; add egg and rest of ingredients. Add raisins and liquid last. Makes 2 small loaves. Bake at 350° for about 45 minutes. NOTE: This is a moist bread that keeps a long time under refrigeration.

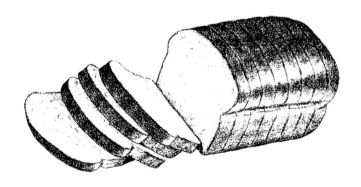

Buttermilk Scones

1 C. buttermilk
2½ C. flour

2 tsp. pure baking soda
Salt

Dissolve the soda in 2 T. of buttermilk. Mix the flour into the rest of the buttermilk until a soft dough is formed. Add a good pinch of salt and the soda; mix very well. Turn out onto a floured board on table; roll lightly and cut into 2-inch scones. Put onto a lightly greased baking sheet and bake in a hot oven, 400° for 15 minutes. Serve hot, split with butter.

Corn Fritters

8 ears corn or 1 pkg. frozen corn
1 egg
1 T. flour

1 C. milk
3 tsp. baking powder
½ tsp. salt

Scrape corn from ears, mix egg and flour together. Add remaining ingredients. Drop by tablespoons on griddle, using bacon grease to fry. Serve with maple syrup.

12-Inch Cast Iron Skillet Corn Bread

1½ C. cornmeal
½ C. flour
1 egg (beaten)
1 tsp. salt

1½ C. milk
4 tsp. baking powder
1 tsp. sugar
2 T. melted shortening

Mix all dry ingredients. Add milk, egg, and shortening. Bake in greased muffin tins or cast iron skillet for 20 minutes or brown crusted.

18

Heavenly Hash

1 (13½ oz.) can crushed pineapple
& juice
½ pkg. miniature marshmallows

1 large pkg. cream cheese
½ pt. whipping cream (whipped)
Chopped pecans

2 or 3 hours ahead of time or night before, combine pineapple, juice and all and marshmallows, till marshmallows are soft. Mash the cheese and add. Whip the cream with 2 T. powdered sugar and ½ to ¾ tsp. vanilla. Whip stiff. Fold in with rest of mixture. Makes 8-inch square pan or you can use a pretty bowl.

Fresh Soda Bread

6 C. flour
1 C. buttermilk, sour milk or
fresh milk

1 tsp. soda
1 tsp. salt

Mix all ingredients together in a basin and make a well in the center. Add enough milk to make a thick dough. Stir with a wooden spoon. The mixture should be slack but not wet and the mixing done lightly and quickly. Add a little more milk if it seems too stiff. With floured hands, put on a lightly floured board or table and flatten the dough into a circle about 1½-inches. Put onto baking sheet and make a large cross over it with a floured knife. Bake in a moderate to hot oven, 375°-400° for about 40 minutes. To keep the bread soft, it is wrapped up in a clean tea towel. For brown bread: 4 C. whole-wheat flour, 2 C. white flour, and a little more milk. The rest is the same.

Ma's Dutch Apple Bread

½ C. shortening (no butter)
1 C. granulated sugar
2 eggs
1 C. coarsely chopped apples
  (peeled)

2 C. all-purpose flour (sifted)
1 ½ T. sour milk
1 tsp. baking soda
½ tsp. salt
1 tsp. vanilla

Cream shortening and sugar; add the eggs and beat. Add the chopped apples. Add the flour and beat well. Mix the sour milk with the soda. Add to batter. Add the salt and vanilla; beat. Put in two 4x8-inch greased pans. Top with mixture of 2 tablespoons and ½ tsp. cinnamon. Bake at 350° for 50 to 60 minutes. NOTE: Nutmeats may also be added.

CORNBREAD

1 ½ C. cornmeal (yellow)
3 tsp. baking powder
½ tsp. soda

½ C. flour
1 tsp. salt
1 T. sugar

Mix above ingredients together and cut in ¼ C. soft oleo. Add all at once, 1 ½ C. buttermilk and 1 egg, well beaten. Pour into hot greased pan. Bake at 500° for 20 to 25 minutes.

PUFFY PANCAKES

4 eggs (slightly beaten)   1 C. milk
1 C. flour

Mix above ingredients together with eggbeater. Add the above mixture to
⅓ C. oleo which has been melted in 9x13-inch pan. (The oleo can be melted
as you preheat the oven at 400°.) Sift 4 T. powdered sugar over top and
bake at 400° until puffy and light brown, approximately 15 minutes. These
do not need to be served with syrup.

Cherry-Nut Christmas Crock

1 lb. butter   ½ tsp. baking soda
3 C. sugar   ½ tsp. salt
5 eggs (separated)   1 tsp. vanilla
1 C. buttermilk   3 (10 oz.) bottles maraschino
5 C. all-purpose flour   cherries
                                  1 lb. whole Brazil nuts or walnuts

Cream butter and sugar. Add beaten egg yolks. Add buttermilk and
flour/soda/salt mixture alternately. Add vanilla. Fold in stiffly beaten egg whites.
Add maraschino cherries, drained of juice (can use red and green cherries).
Add 1 lb. of Brazil nuts or walnuts. Bake in 4 large or 5 small loaf pans for
1 hour at 350°. To prepare pans, grease pan; put layer of brown paper in bottom and grease again. Freezes well.

CORN BREAD

1 can cream-style corn   1 tsp. salt
1 egg   1 C. cornmeal
⅔ C. milk   1 tsp. soda
¼ C. oil   1 can green chiles (small)

Mix all ingredients well and pour into 8x8-inch greased pan. Cover with 1
or 2 C. sharp Cheddar cheese. Bake at 375° for 40 to 45 minutes. (Be sure
the peppers or chiles are mixed in very well.)

"MMMMMMMM" Buns

2 C. lukewarm water
3 pkgs. dry yeast
1 stick margarine (melted)
1½ tsp. salt

⅓ C. sugar
2 eggs
6½ C. all-purpose flour

Dissolve yeast in lukewarm water. Add salt, sugar, melted margarine, and 2 T. flour. Beat well with electric beater. Add eggs and beat again with spoon, add the rest of flour gradually. Let rest for 30 minutes or until dough is doubled in size. Shape into buns. Let rise until doubled. Bake at 350° until brown. This is a good recipe for cinnamon rolls and raised doughnuts.

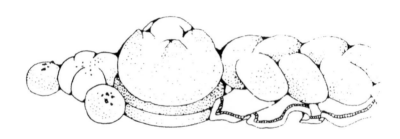

ANGEL BISCUITS

5 C. flour
1 tsp. baking soda
1 tsp. salt
3 tsp. baking powder
3 T. sugar

¾ C. shortening
1 pkg. yeast, dissolved in
  ½ C. lukewarm milk
2 C. buttermilk

Put in refrigerator until ready to use. Roll out dough rather thick. Bake at 400° for 12 minutes.

CINNAMON-NUT COFFEE RING

1 loaf bread dough (thawed)
1 stick butter or margarine
½ C. sugar

2 tsp. cinnamon
½ C. nuts

Let dough set out for 1 hour till room temperature, then flour surface. Roll and push dough into a 14x8-inch rectange. Spread dough with all but 2 T. of the butter. Fold entire rectange into thirds. Roll out again and fold again. Let dough rest for 10 minutes. Roll out one more time, then spread remaining butter on dough and sprinkle sugar, cinnamon, and nuts on dough. Roll dough jelly roll fashion from long side. Place seam side down on greased jelly roll pan and shape into circle, pinching the seam well to seal. Using scissors, make deep cuts from outside almost to center, 1-inch apart. Turn each section cut side up so filling shows. Cover and let rise till double, about 1 hour. Bake at 350° for 25 minutes. Cool and drizzle with a glaze of ½ C. powdered sugar and 1 T. milk.

Oatmeal Crackers

1⅓ C. whole wheat flour
1⅔ C. oatmeal
½ tsp. baking soda
2 T. sugar

½ tsp. baking powder
⅔ C. skim milk
¾ tsp. lemon juice
6 T. margarine (soft)

Mix dry ingredients (save ⅔ C. oatmeal to roll with). Add rest of ingredients. Divide dough in half. Cover and refrigerate 10 to 30 minutes. Roll dough out ½ at a time. Cut into 2-inch squares. Cut squares in half (forms a triangle). Prick with fork and bake at 400° for 8 minutes or until dry and golden.

MARSHMALLOW ROLLS

¼ C. sugar
1 tsp. cinnamon
2 cans of 8 oz. Pillsbury cresent
dinner refrigerator rolls

16 large marshmallows
¼ C. chopped nuts (optional)

ICING:
½ C. powdered sugar
2 to 3 tsp. milk

½ tsp. vanilla

Combine sugar and cinnamon. Separate 2 cans cresent dough in 16 triangles. Dip a marshmallow in melted butter, then in sugar-cinnamon mixture. Place marshmallows on wide end of triangle. Fold corners over marshmallows and roll toward point, completely covering marshmallows and squeeze edges of dough to seal. Dip point-side in butter and place buttered side down in greased deep muffin pans. Repeat with remaining marshmallows. Place pan on cookie sheet during baking. Bake for 10 to 15 minutes at 375° or until golden brown. While yet warm remove from pan and drizzle with icing. Sprinkle with nuts, if desired. Makes 16 rolls.

Garden Rhubarb Muffins

1¼ C. brown sugar
½ C. cooking oil
1 egg
2 tsp. vanilla
1½ C. rhubarb (diced fine)
1 C. buttermilk

½ C. nuts
¼ tsp. walnut flavoring
2½ C. all-purpose flour
1 tsp. baking soda
1 tsp. baking powder
½ tsp. salt

TOPPING:
1 tsp. melted butter
⅓ C. sugar

1 tsp. cinnamon

Mix all ingredients together. Pour into muffin cups. Mix the topping and sprinkle on top of each muffin. Makes 12 to 18 muffins. Bake at 375° for 20 to 25 minutes.

CARROT-BANANA BREAD

½ C. butter
1 C. brown sugar
2 eggs
1 C. mashed bananas (3 med. size)
2 C. all-purpose flour
1 tsp. baking soda

½ tsp. baking powder
½ tsp. cinnamon
¼ tsp. salt
1 C. grated carrots
½ C. chopped nuts

Cream butter with sugar; beat in eggs. Mash bananas in small bowl. Mix flour, soda, baking powder, cinnamon, and salt. Mix flour mixture alternately with bananas. Combine with egg, butter, and sugar mixture. Stir in carrots and nuts. Bake in a greased 9x5x3-inch loaf pan at 350° for 50 to 60 minutes until done.. Cool for 10 minutes, turn out of pan and cool completely.

BANANA NUT BREAD

1 C. sugar
½ C. oleo
2 eggs
3 ripe bananas
1⅓ C. flour

½ tsp. baking powder
1 tsp. soda
¾ C. walnuts, black or English
Salt, ½ tsp. if desired

Mix first 4 ingredients in blender. Pour into bowl and add dry ingredients, sifted together. Mix well and add nuts. Bake at 325° to 350° for 1 hour in bread loaf pan.

BLUEBERRY MUFFINS

¾ C. sugar
¼ C. butter
¼ C. shortening
2 eggs (separated)
2⅓ C. flour

2 tsp. baking powder
½ tsp. salt
1 C. milk
1 C. blueberries

Cream sugar, butter, and shortening, Add egg yolks and mix well. Stir dry ingredients together and reserve ½ cup. Stir dry ingredients into creamed mixture alternately with milk. Stir until all ingredients are moistened. Fold in stiffly beaten egg whites. Combine blueberries with the ½ C. dry ingredients and fold into batter. Fill greased or paper-lined muffin cups ⅔ full. Bake at 400° for 20 to 30 minutes. Yields: 1½ dozen. (The blueberries can be frozen or canned. Drain them well.)

BANANA BREAD

1 C. sugar
½ C. Crisco
1 C. mashed bananas
2 eggs
½ tsp. soda, dissolved in 1 T. warm water

1½ C. flour
1 tsp. baking powder
¼ tsp. salt
1 tsp. vanilla

Cream sugar and Crisco; add eggs. Add bananas then dry ingredients. Add vanilla and bake in two small greased loaf pans at 350° for ½ hour.

DONUT MUFFINS

½ C. sugar
¼ C. melted oleo
1 egg
½ C. milk
¾ tsp. nutmeg

1 tsp. baking powder
1 C. flour
¼ C. melted butter
½ C. sugar
1 tsp. cinnamon

Mix all ingredients with the exception of the last three. Place in a 12 compartment greased muffin tin. Bake at 375° for 15 to 20 minutes. Turn out and dip in melted butter and then mixture of sugar and cinnamon.

PEANUT BUTTER MUFFINS

1¾ C. flour
½ tsp. salt
2 tsp. baking powder

¼ C. sugar
¾ C. milk
1 egg

Mix together flour, salt, baking powder, and sugar. Beat together milk and egg. Melt together ¼ C. shortening and ½ C. peanut butter in the microwave for 1 minute on full power. Mix in milk and egg mixture. Bake at 400° for 25 minutes.

ALL BRAN BROWN BREAD

2 C. all-bran
2 C. buttermilk or sour milk
2 tsp. soda
1 C. sugar

1 T. molasses or syrup
2 C. flour
1 tsp. salt
1 C. raisins

Soak all-bran in buttermilk for 15 minutes. Mix all together. Bake at 350° for 1 hour.

PUMPKIN BREAD

3 C. sugar
1 C. salad oil
4 eggs (beaten)
1 lb. can pumpkin
⅔ C. water
3½ C. flour
2 tsp. soda

2 tsp. salt
1 tsp. baking powder
1 tsp. nutmeg
1 tsp. allspice
1 tsp. cinnamon
½ tsp. cloves

Cream sugar and oil. Add eggs and pumpkin, mix. Sift dry ingredients. Add alternately with water. Pour into 2 well-greased and floured 9x5-inch loaf pans. Bake at 350° for 1½ hours. Stand for 10 minutes and then remove from pan and cool.

PUMPKIN BREAD

3 C. sugar
3⅓ C. flour
½ tsp. baking powder
2 tsp. soda
1½ tsp. salt
½ tsp. ground cloves
1 tsp. cinnamon
1 C. salad oil
1 C. water
2 C. pumpkin
4 eggs

Put ingredients in large mixing bowl and mix well. Pour into 2 greased and floured loaf pans. Bake at 325° for 1 hour and 20 minutes.

SWEET MUFFINS

1 egg
½ C. milk
¼ C. salad oil
1½ C. flour
½ C. sugar
2 tsp. baking powder
½ tsp. salt

Heat oven to 400°. Grease bottoms of 12 medium muffin cups. Beat egg and stir in milk and oil. Mix in remaining ingredients just until flour is moistened. Batter should be lumpy. Fill muffin cups two-thirds full. Bake for 20 to 25 minutes or until golden brown. Immediately remove from pan.

RAISED VET BOLLEN

2 3/8 C. warm water
2 T. Realemon juice
1/8 lb. or 2 dry yeast
1 C. sugar
2 tsp. salt
1 tsp. nutmeg
½ C. dry milk
⅔ C. oil
4 eggs
8 C. flour
2 C. washed raisins

Let raise for 45 minutes. Drop spoonful into hot fat using deep fat fryer. Drop into glaze.

YEAST DONUTS

2 C. milk (scalded & cooled)
1 pkg. yeast, dissolved in
  ¼ C. warm water
½ C. sugar
½ T. vanilla
1 egg
5-6½ C. flour

½ C. oleo
1 tsp. salt
Dash of nutmeg
½ tsp. soda
½ T. lemon juice
1 T. baking powder

Add oleo, salt, sugar, nutmeg, and lemon juice. When cool, add yeast mixture, beaten eggs, and vanilla. Add 2¼ C. flour, soda, and baking powder. Mix with mixer. Gradually add flour; dough will be soft. Refrigerate overnight in tightly covered container. Roll or pat out dough to ½-inch thick. Let rise for 10 minutes. Fry in hot oil; drain. Glaze or sugar while hot. Mixture will keep for several days in refrigerator.

ENGLISH MUFFIN LOAF

1 pkg. yeast
3 C. flour
½ T. sugar
1 tsp. salt

1 C. milk
1/8 tsp. baking soda
¼ C. water
Cornmeal

Combine 1½ C. flour, yeast, sugar, salt, and soda. Heat liquids until very warm, 120° to 130°; add to dry mixture and beat well. Stir in rest of flour to make a stiff batter. Grease pan and sprinkle with cornmeal. Cover and let rise in warm place for 45 minutes. Bake at 400° for 25 minutes. Slice and toast.

POCKET BREAD

1 pkg. active dry yeast
1⅓ C. warm water
1 tsp. salt
¼ tsp. sugar

1 T. oil
3 to 3½ C. all-purpose flour
Cornmeal

Dissolve yeast in warm water in large bowl. Stir in salt, sugar, oil, and 1½ C. of flour. Beat until smooth. Stir in enough of remaining flour to make dough easy to handle. Turn dough onto lightly floured surface. Knead until smooth and elastic, about 10 minutes. Place in greased bowl, turn greased side up. Cover and let rise in a warm place until double (1 hour). Dough is ready when indent remains when touched. Divide into 6 equal parts. Shape into balls and let rise for 30 minutes. Sprinkle ungreased cookie sheets with cornmeal. Roll each ball into circle 1/8-inch thick. Place 2 circles in opposite corners of cookie sheets and let rise for 30 minutes. Heat oven to 500°. Bake until loaves are puffed and light brown (10 minutes). Tear each loaf crosswise into halves. Fill with taco filling, cheese, lettuce or with any meat filling. Serve immediately or place hot unfilled loaves in plastic bags to keep moist and pliable until ready to serve.

RHUBARB BREAD

1 egg (beaten)
1 C. sour milk
1 tsp. salt
1 tsp. soda
1½ C. brown sugar

1 tsp. vanilla
2½ C. flour
1½ C. diced rhubarb
⅔ C. oil

Mix in order given. Divide batter between 2 loaf pans (8x4-inch). Mix ½ C. white sugar and 1 T. butter and sprinkle over top of batter. Bake at 325° for 1 hour. Don't overbake.

APRICOT BREAD

2 C. dried apricots (cut-up)

Cover with boiling water and set 1½ hours; drain.

2 C. sugar	4 T. shortening
2 eggs	1½ C. orange juice
4 C. flour	½ tsp. soda
4 tsp. baking powder	1 C. nutmeats

Mix all ingredients and put in 2 loaf pans. Let raise if you wish, 20 minutes. Bake for 55 to 65 minutes at 375°.

HEALTH BREAD

¾ C. milk	4-4½ C. unbleached flour
¼ C. sugar	1 C. whole-wheat flour
1 T. salt	½ C. rye flour
¼-½ C. instant non-fat dry milk	1 C. wheat germ
⅓ C. oleo	1 egg white (beaten)
1½ C. warm water	1 T. cold water
2 pkgs. dry yeast	Sesame seeds

Scald milk. Stir in sugar, salt, dry milk, and oleo. Cool to lukewarm. Sprinkle yeast in warm water and stir to dissolve. Combine milk mixture, yeast, water, and flours. Knead for 8 to 10 minutes. Let rise about 1 hour. Punch down and shape into 4 round loaves. Place 2 loaves on one greased baking pan. Cover and let rise till doubled (about 50 minutes). Bake at 400° for 10 minutes and then brush tops with combined egg white and water. Sprinkle on seeds and bake 10 more minutes or till done. This recipes makes four small loaves of bread. It is nutritious and has a fine texture.

PINWHEEL BREAD

2 pkgs. active dry yeast
2 C. warm water
2 C. milk
½ C. sugar
½ C. shortening

2 T. salt
8½ C. flour
¼ C. molasses
4 to 4½ C. whole-wheat flour

In large mixing bowl, dissolve yeast in warm water. In saucepan heat milk, sugar, shortening, and salt just till warm, stirring constantly till shortening almost melts. Add to yeast mixture in mixing bowl. Stir in 4 C. of all purpose flour and beat till smooth. Cover and let rise in a warm place for 1 hour. Stir batter down and turn about ½ of batter into another bowl. To half of batter, stir in enough of remaining all-purpose flour to make moderately stiff dough. On floured surface, knead 6 to 8 minutes or till smooth and elastic. Place in greased bowl, turning once to grease surface and cover. To remaining batter, stir in molasses till well blended. Add enough whole-wheat flour to make moderately stiff dough. Knead for 6 to 8 minutes. Place one dark portion atop one light portion. Roll-up tightly into loaf, beginning at short end. Place loaf in greased 9x5x3-inch pan. Repeat with the rest, cover and let rise for 45 to 60 minutes or till double. Bake in 375° oven for 30 to 35 minutes. Cover with foil after 20 minutes to prevent top from over browning. Remove from pans, cool and store in plastic bags.

DATE NUT BREAD

1½ C. boiling water
1 lb. dates (cut-up)
1 tsp. (heaping) baking soda
¾ C. nutmeats
1½ C. brown sugar
¾ C. shortening

2 medium-sized eggs
3 C. flour
1½ tsp. maple flavoring
½ tsp. salt
1½ tsp. vanilla

Pour water over dates, soda, and nuts; let stand until lukewarm. Cream sugar, shortening, and eggs; beat well. Add flavorings. Bake at 350° for 1 hour. This recipe makes two large loaves. This is good at Christmas or anytime.

HOLIDAY BREAD

Makes 3 to 4 loaves or 9 to 10 cans. Boil 1 pkg. white seedless raisins in 2¼ C. water for 15 minutes. Chop and add 1 lb. dates to raisins. Mix together the following:

4 T. shortening	4 tsp. soda
2 C. sugar	1 tsp. salt
2 eggs	32 maraschino cherries
1 tsp. vanilla	1 No. 2 can crushed pineapple
5½ C. flour	1 C. chopped nuts

Add date and raisin mixture. Bake in greased loaf pan or cans. Fill can ½ full. Bake at 350° for 45 to 60 minutes. Test with toothpick.

THIN BREAD

2½ C. flour	1 tsp. baking powder
2 tsp. sugar	

Stir the above ingredients together and add ½ C. lukewarm water and ¼ C. cooking oil. Mix till dough can be gathered into a ball. (Add more water, if needed.) Let dough rest for 15 minutes. Divide into 10 portions. With a rolling pin, roll each portion into an 8½-inch circle. Place on lightly greased cookie sheet. Bake at 450° for 7 minutes. These are like crackers only better.

CAKES

PEANUT GOODIES

Preheat oven to 350°.

CAKE:

2 C. flour	1 C. sugar
2 tsp. baking powder	1 C. hot water

Mix well, then add 1 egg and 1 tsp. vanilla. Put in greased and floured 11¼x7½x1½-inch pan and bake. Cool cake and cut into squares. Make a powdered sugar frosting that is runny. Ground a medium bag of peanuts in blender or meat chopper. Roll square in frosting on all sides, then the peanuts.

ROLL IN ONE CAKE

1 can cherry pie filling	¾ C. flour
5 eggs (separated)	¾ C. sugar
¾ T. cream of tartar	

Spread pie filling in greased 15x10x1-inch jelly roll pan to within 1-inch of edge, reserving ¼ cup for topping. In large mixing bowl beat egg whites with cream of tartar and salt at high speed of mixer until stiff peaks form. Gradually add sugar and the egg yolks, beating at high speed until well blended. At low speed add flour mixing just until flour is blended in. Pour over pie filling, spreading carefully to cover. Bake at 375° for 18 to 20 minutes, until light golden brown. Loosen edges and turn out immediately onto a cloth sprinkled with confectioner's sugar. Roll up and cool. Serve plain or with topping of ¼ C. pie filling with 1 C. sweetened dairy sour cream or whipped cream.

GERMAN CHOCOLATE CAKE

1 (19½ oz.) box yellow or white	3 eggs (separated)
1 (3¾ oz.) box chocolate or fudge	1 C. milk
instant pudding mix	1 C. sugar plus
2 C. milk	1½ T. cornstarch
¼ C. oil	1 tsp. vanilla
	1 C. coconut

Before getting beaters dirty, beat the egg whites until stiff in small bowl and set aside. Then using same beaters and a large mixing bowl, mix the dry cake and pudding mixes, 2 C. milk, and the oil. Beat until fluffy. Gradually add the beaten egg whites. Mix well and pour into a greased 9x13-inch Pan. Bake at 350° for 45 minutes.

For Frosting: Beat 3 egg yolks and stir in milk, sugar, and cornstarch which was mixed together, vanilla and coconut. Cook until thick on low heat, stirring constantly. Pour over cooled cake.

FRUIT COCKTAIL CAKE

2 C. flour
1½ C. sugar
1 tsp. soda
1 tsp. salt
2 eggs

1 can fruit cocktail
 (juice & all)
½ C. coconut
½ C. brown sugar

Sift together first four ingredients; add eggs and fruit cocktail and pour into well-greased 9x13-inch pan. Over batter sprinkle coconut and brown sugar. Bake at 375° for 40 to 50 minutes.

FROSTING:
¾ C. sugar
½ C. evaporated milk

1 stick oleo
1 tsp. vanilla

Bring all ingredients to a boil. Continue boiling for 2 minutes. Pour over cake as soon as it comes from the oven.

VELVET CAKE LAYERS

1 C. shortening
2 C. sugar
4 eggs
3 C. cake flour

2 tsp. baking powder
½ tsp. salt
1 C. milk
1 tsp. vanilla

Cream shortening and sugar. Add eggs, 1 at a time beating after each. Sift together flour, baking powder, and salt. Add and alternate with milk to creamed mixture. Add vanilla and bake in 2 greased 9-inch layer pans. Bake at 375° for 35 minutes. Cool and remove from pans; frost to taste.

BANANA CAKE

3 C. cake flour
2 C. sugar
1 C. chopped walnuts
1½ C. bananas (blended)
¾ C. oil
1 tsp. soda

1 tsp. salt
1 tsp. cinnamon
1 tsp. vanilla
3 eggs
1 (8 oz.) can crushed pineapple
 (including juice)

Mix cake flour and sugar well, then add all the rest of the ingredients. Beat well and pour into 2 round pans. Bake at 350° for 35 to 40 minutes. Makes nice cup cakes, too. Frost with 1 pkg. cream cheese and 3½ C. powdered sugar.

QUICK AND EASY FUDGE CAKE

1 chocolate cake mix (dark fudge)
1 pkg. instant chocolate pudding
  mix
1 large pkg. chocolate chips
2 eggs
1¾ C. milk

Stir all together with a spoon. Grease and flour a bundt cake pan. Bake at 350° for 50 to 55 minutes. Cool and remove from pan. Dust with powdered sugar.

SUNSHINE CAKE

Beat 1 C. sugar with 7 egg yolks for 8 minutes. Add 1 C. flour and 4 T. water, 1 tsp. vanilla, and ¼ tsp. lemon flavoring. Beat 7 egg whites, ½ tsp. salt, ½ tsp. cream of tartar until stiff and egg whites form peaks. Add ¾ C. sugar and fold in carefully. Combine the egg mixture with the egg white mixture and pour into a tube cake pan (angel food pan). Bake at 325° for about 50 to 60 minutes. If you like spice flavor cake, add 1 tsp. cinnamon, ¼ tsp. nutmeg, and ¼ tsp. allspice.

ICE BOX CAKE

CRUST:
½ C. graham crackers or vanilla wafers (crushed)

1ST LAYER:
½ of crumbs

2ND LAYER:
1½ C. powdered sugar   ½ C. butter
2 eggs

Beat all together

3RD LAYER:
Whip 1 cup of cream and add a flat can of crushed pineapple and ½ C. chopped nuts. Cover with rest of crumbs and refrigerate overnight.

FRUIT CAKE

1 C. sugar   1 tsp. soda
¼ tsp. salt   1 C. flour (sifted)

Mix together above. Drain off juice and beat together with spoon:

1 egg   2 C. fruit cocktail

Then fold in the other ingredients. Put on top ½ C. brown sugar, ½ C. nuts, bake in slow oven for 1 hour and 10 minutes.

BLUEBERRY STREUSEL COFFEE CAKE

2¾ C. flour
1½ tsp. double acting baking powder
1½ tsp. baking soda
1 tsp. salt

¾ C. softened butter
1 C. sugar
3 eggs
16 oz. container sour cream
2 tsp. vanilla

STREUSEL:
¾ C. brown sugar
¾ C. chopped walnuts

1 tsp. cinnamon
2 C. blueberries

Preheat oven to 375°. Grease and flour a 10-inch tube pan. Combine flour, baking powder, soda, and salt; set aside. In large bowl, cream butter, and sugar at medium speed till light and fluffy. Add eggs, 1 at a time - beating well after each addition. Add flour mixture alternately with sour cream and vanilla. Combine streusel ingredients; set aside ½ cup. Toss remaining with berries. Spread ⅓ of batter in pan. Sprinkle ½ of berry mixture over and spread another ⅓ batter and sprinkle with remaining berries. Top with remaining batter. Sprinkle on reserve streusel. Bake for 60 to 65 minutes or till toothpick comes out clean. Cool in pan on wire rack for 10 minutes. Remove from pan. Makes 16 servings.

SPRING FLING CAKE

1 pkg. yellow cake mix or
  butter brickle
1 (11 oz.) can undrained
  mandarin oranges

1 tsp. burnt sugar flavoring
4 eggs
½ C. oil

Combine in a bowl with a spoon and mix with a mixer for 2 to 3 minutes.
Bake in 9x13-inch greased pan for 20 to 25 minutes.

TOPPING:
Prepare while cake is baking the following:

1 (15½ oz.) can or smaller
  undrained pineapple
1 box vanilla instant pudding (dry)

¼ tsp. lemon flavoring
¼ tsp. pineapple flavoring

Mix together and add 9 oz. of whipped topping. Spread on a slightly cooled
cake and keep cool.

MOLASSES CAKE

½ C. lard
1 egg
1½ C. sugar
1 C. molasses
1½ C. sour milk
1½ tsp. cloves

3 level tsp. cinnamon
1 level tsp. nutmeg
3 C. flour
1 C. raisins
1½ tsp. soda

Mix and put in a 9x13-inch pan and bake at 350° for 40 to 50 minutes or
until a toothpick comes out clean.

CANDY

PEANUT BRITTLE

2 C. sugar   ½ C. water
1 C. white corn syrup

Combine in a 3-quart pan and cook till soft ball stage. (If you have no candy thermometer - till mixture is stringy, about 2-4 inches long from wooden spoon.) Then add 1 pkg. Raw Spanish Peanuts. Stir till crack stage or (when foam turns a deep golden brown). Then quickly add:

½ tsp. salt   1 tsp. vanilla
1 tsp. baking soda   1 T. butter

Stir quickly and fast. Spread on 2 buttered cookie sheets. Do it quickly as candy hardens in the pan within 15 to 20 seconds. Spread thin. After 3 to 4 minutes take wax paper and spread to the edges of the pan. Then put in a cold place for 10 to 30 minutes. Break in pieces and store in a closed container in a cool place. Coffee cans or Tupperware works nicely. Have all ingredients ready and measured before you start making the candy.

ORANGE COCONUT BALLS

½ pkg. vanilla wafers (crushed)   ½ C. margarine
3-4 C. Rice Krispies   (softened)
1 lb. pkg. powdered sugar   ½ C. chopped pecans
1 (6 oz.) can frozen orange juice   Flaked coconut
    concentrate (thawed)

In mixing bowl, combine vanilla wafer crumbs, rice cereal, powdered sugar, orange juice concentrate, margarine, and pecans; mix well. Form mixture into balls. Roll in coconut and place on baking sheets to set.

CARAMEL CORN

6 qts. popcorn

Boil the following for 5 minutes, stirring occasionally:

2 C. brown sugar	1 tsp. soda
2 sticks butter	1 tsp. salt
½ C. white syrup	

Remove from fire and pour over corn. Add 1 C. nuts immediately. Coat well and bake at 200° for 1 hour, stirring every 15 minutes.

Variation: Ruthy uses ¼ tsp. cream of tartar.

TWO-LAYER CANDY

1 C. sugar	2 C. sugar
1 C. packed brown sugar	¾ C. light cream
½ C. light cream	10 large marshmallows
1 T. corn syrup	½ C. margarine
1 T. butter	1 (6 oz.) pkg. semi-sweet
1 tsp. vanilla	chocolate chips
½ C. chopped nuts	

In saucepan, combine the 1 C. of sugar, brown sugar, ½ C. cream, corn syrup, and butter. Cook to soft ball stage (234° on candy thermometer). Remove from heat and let stand until lukewarm. Beat vigorously until creamy; stir in vanilla and nuts. Pour in 9x9x2-inch baking pan. In saucepan, combine the 2 C. sugar, ¾ C. cream, and marshmallows. Cook to softball stage. Remove from heat and stir in margarine and chocolate chips. Beat until creamy. Pour over first layer in pan. Cool and cut into squares.

SYRUP CANDY

(This recipe came from Holland with Tunis's mother. They even used it to soothe sore throats.)

1 C. white sugar   1 T. vinegar
1 C. Karo syrup (dark)

Cook for 10 to 15 minutes to soft crack stage. Cool to where you can touch it. Butter hands well and pull and stretch until candy is of a smooth taffy consistency. Cut in pieces with knife or scissors.

MOUNDS CANDY

Mix 1 stick softened oleo, 1 can Eagle Brand milk, and 2 lbs. powdered sugar until smooth. Add 14 oz. coconut and 2 tsp. coconut flavoring. Shape as desired. Place on waxed paper overnight and put in refrigerator.

For Coating: Melt 1-inch square parafin in double boiler. Add 12 oz. chocolate chips. Dip balls and lay on wax paper with a fork.

CHERRY-CHOCOLATE CANDY

2 C. sugar   1 tsp. vanilla
⅔ C. evaporated milk   10 oz. crushed salted peanuts
Dash of salt   (blender works very well)
12 regular marshmallows   ¾ C. peanut butter
½ C. margarine   1 T. margarine
6 oz. cherry baking chips   12 oz. chocolate chips

Combine sugar, milk, salt, marshmallows, and ½ C. margarine in saucepan over medium heat. Boil 5 minutes. Remove from heat. Add cherry chips and vanilla. Pour into 9x13-inch buttered pan. Melt chocolate baking chips in double boiler. Add peanut butter, 1 T. margarine, and crushed salted peanuts. Spread over cherry mixture and chill. Cut into small pieces to serve.

MARTHA WASHINGTON CHOCOLATES

½ lb. butter
1 can Eagle Brand milk
2 tsp. vanilla

2 pkgs. powdered sugar
  (two 1-lb. boxes)
½ pkg. fine coconut (4 oz.)

Combine in mixing bowl and refrigerate until you can handle; approximately 6 to 8 hours. Melt in double boiler:

¼ lb. paraffin

2 (6 oz. ea.) pkgs. chocolate
  chips

Use toothpicks to dip balls into chocolate. Can be frozen.

MASHED POTATO CANDY

¾ C. mashed potatoes
4 C. powdered sugar

4 C. coconut
1 tsp. vanilla

Mix above and roll into walnut-sized balls. Put on cookie sheet in freezer overnight. Now mix ½ bar of paraffin and a 12 oz. pkg. chocolate chips in double boiler. Dip cold balls in chocolate. Almonds can be added to top of each ball before freezing if desired. This makes them taste like Almond Joy candy bars. (Marla says that she always makes a double batch, as they go fast.)

PISTACHIO CANDY

1 lb. powdered sugar
1 pkg. Pistachio pudding

5 T. cream (can use milk)
¼ C. butter

Mix powdered sugar and pudding; add cream and butter. Mix by hand or knead by hand until thoroughly mixed. (Do not use mixer.) Put in 9x5x3-inch pan. Let set for 30 minutes and cut into small squares.

MAIN DISHES

SCALLOPED EGGS AND HAM

¼ C. butter
4¼ C. flour
½ tsp. salt

1/8 tsp. paprika
Pepper
2 C. milk

Cook this to make white sauce:

6 hard-boiled eggs

1 C. cubed ham

Alternate layers of egg, ham, and green pepper, if desired and the white sauce. Heat ½ C. fine bread crumbs; mix with 2 T. butter and 3 T. of grated cheese. Put on top and bake at 350° for about 25 minutes. Makes 4 to 6 servings.

HEARTY BEEF 'N' CHEESE CRESCENT PIE

1¼ lbs. ground beef
¼ C. chopped green pepper
8 oz. can cut green beans
   (drained)
¼ tsp. cumin seed (optional)
¼ to ½ tsp. salt & paprika
1 can (8 oz.) Pillsbury refrigerted
   quick crescent dinner rolls

2 C. (8 oz.) shredded Monterey
   Jack or Cheddar cheese
⅓ C. chopped onion
8 oz. can (1 C.) tomato sauce
   with mushrooms
¼ tsp. garlic salt
1 egg (slightly beaten)

Preheat oven to 375°. In a large fry pan, brown ground beef, onion, and green pepper; drain fat. Stir in tomato sauce, beans, cumin seed, and garlic salt; simmer while preparing crust. Separate crescent dough into 8 triangles. Place triangles in ungreased 9-inch pie pan; press over bottom and on sides to form crust. Combine egg and 1 C. cheese; spread over crust. Spoon hot meat mixture into crust. Sprinkle with remaining cheese and paprika. Bake for 20 to 25 minutes. For easier serving, let stand for 5 minutes before cutting into wedges. Makes 5 to 6 servings.

CREAMED EGGS

WHITE SAUCE:
½ stick butter
Pepper, to taste

¼ C. flour
2 C. milk

Add to white sauce 2 chicken bouillon cubes, 3 to 4 oz. Velveeta cheese, and 6 to 8 hard-boiled eggs that have been cubed to bite-size. Simmer for 10 minutes and serve over toast.

CHEESE STRATA

12 slices white bread
¾ lb. sharp American
   (sliced cheese)
2 C. finely diced ham
6 slightly beaten eggs

2 T. onion
3½ C. milk
½ tsp. salt
¼ tsp. dry mustard

Cut bread in squares, removing the crusts. Fill in the bottom with bread. Place a cheese layer, a ham layer, and then a bread layer. Pour remaining ingredients over all. Cover and refrigerate at least 6 hours. Bake, uncovered at 325° for 55 minutes. For a finished look, sprinkle with shredded cheese 5 minutes before end of baking time. Let stand for 10 minutes before cutting. Serves 12.

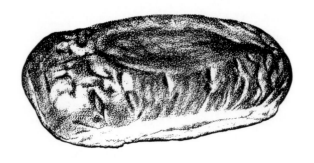

SPAGHETTI CASSEROLE

Brown 1 lb. hamburger and 1 onion in 2 T. butter. Add ½ T. Sloppy Joe mix, frozen mixed vegetables (1 box, cooked a little), and 1 can spaghetti. Bake at 350° for 30 minutes.

BACON AND CHEESE OVEN OMELET

12 slices of bacon
8 eggs (beaten)

6 slices cheese
1 C. milk

Cook bacon and drain, curl 1 slice, chop 4 slices, and leave others whole. Arrange cheese in bottom of buttered 9-inch pie pan. Beat together eggs and milk. Add chopped bacon, Pour over cheese and bake for 30 minutes in 350° oven. Arrange whole bacon on top around curl. Bake 10 minutes longer. Let stand 5 minutes before cutting.

BAKED EGGS

6 eggs (slightly beaten)
⅓ C. shredded Cheddar cheese or
   Velveeta

⅔ C. milk
Salt & pepper

Melt quarter stick of oleo in 8x8-inch glass pan. Add above ingredients and stir. Bake at 350° for 15 to 20 minutes. Cut in squares. (I melt the cheese in the milk first. This recipe can be doubled and put in a 9x12-inch pan.)

PIGS IN BLANKETS

CRUST:

1 C. shortening

½ tsp. salt

2 eggs

1 T. sugar

1 C. milk

2 tsp. baking powder

3 C. flour

Cut shortening into dry ingredients. Add milk and mix. This is a soft dough. Roll out on a well floured surface. Shape seasoned sausage into logs 2 or 3 inches long and seal inside dough. Bake at 375° for 30 minutes.

LASAGNA

1 lb. sweet Italian sausage

½ lb. ground beef

1 T. whole basil

Salt

1 (1 lb.) can stewed tomatoes

2 cans (6 oz. ea.) tomato paste

6 large, wide lasagna noodles

1 tsp. olive oil

CHEESE FILLING:

2 C. cottage cheese

½ C. grated Parmesan cheese

2 T. parsley

2 eggs (beaten)

2 tsp. salt

½ tsp. pepper

Brown meats and add basil, 1½ tsp. salt, 1 C. water, stewed tomatoes, and paste. Bring to boil and simmer, stirring occasionally for 30 minutes. Cook noodles in boiling salted water with olive oil. Drain and arrange half in greased 13x9x2-inch dish. Spread with half the filling, then half of the cheese filling. Repeat layers. Bake in moderate (350°) oven for 30 minutes. Let stand for 10 mintues before cutting in squares. May top with sliced mozzarella cheese after a few minutes before removing from the oven.

SCALLOPED POTATOES AND HAM

1 large onion (chopped)
1 (8 oz.) pkg. cream cheese
1 can cream of celery soup
1 can cream of chicken soup

Ham (cubed) (already cooked)
  (as much as you desire)
6 or 8 slices of cheese
1 large pkg. frozen hash brown
  potatoes

Cook chopped onion in small amount of water, to this add cream cheese, celery soup, and chicken soup. Bring to a boil, stirring frequently. Put potatoes in a greased 9x13-inch pan. Put cubed ham over potatoes and cover with sauce. Put foil over baking dish and bake at 350° for 1 hour. Take out of oven and put sliced cheese over top and return uncovered to oven for 15 minutes more. (Ham can be optional if you want just scalloped potatoes.)

FRENCH FRY CASSEROLE

1½ lb. hamburger
¼ C. onion
1 lb. frozen French fries
1 can cream of celery soup

½ can milk
4 oz. Velveeta cheese
1 (10 oz.) pkg. frozen mixed
  vegetables

Season hamburger with salt and pepper. Brown with onion. Put in large flat dish. Cook vegetables and put on top of hamburger; cover with French fries. Heat soup and milk to melt cheese and pour on top. Bake covered at 400° for 15 minutes. Uncovered for 15 minutes at 325°.

AU GRATIN MAIN DISH

8 to 10 C. potatoes
  (cooked & cubed)
1 can cream of mushroom soup
8 oz. container sour cream
¼ C. onion (chopped)

2 (4 oz. ea.) cans mushrooms
  or ½ lb. fresh mushrooms
2 C. cubed Cheddar cheese
2 C. ham (cubed)

Combine ingredients and bake in a casserole or 9x13-inch baking dish for about 1 hour at 300°-325° until heated through and bubbly.

SCALLOPED POTATOES N' FRANKS

8 franks
3 tsp. butter
1½ C. onion
¼ C. flour
3 C. sliced potatoes

1½ tsp. salt
1/8 tsp. pepper
2 C. milk
1 C. Swiss cheese
2 tsp. parsley

In saucepan melt butter, onions, flour, salt, and pepper. Remove from heat and gradually stir in milk. Cook over medium heat and stir in cheese and parsley. Layer half of potatoes in a buttered two quart casserole and pour on half of cheese sauce. Place franks over sauce and repeat with remaining ingredients. Cook and bake at 350° for 1 hour. Remove cover and bake for 15 to 30 minutes.

CORN AND PORK

4 to 6½-inch pork chops
1 T. prepared mustard
1 (1 lb.) can (2 C.) golden cream
    corn
⅔ C. soft bread (cubed)

2 T. onion (chopped)
1 T. green pepper (chopped)
1 tsp. salt
Dash of pepper
½ C. water

Spread pork chops with mustard. Dip in eggs and roll in cracker crumbs; brown well. Combine corn, bread crumbs, onion, green pepper, salt, and pepper. Arrange chops in 1-layer in baking dish. Drain grease from pan and stir in ½ C. water and bring to a boil. Pour over chops. Top with corn mixture, cover and bake at 350° for 15 minutes. Uncover and bake for 45 minutes more.

BACON-GO-AROND

8 slices Canadian-style bacon
    (cut ¼-inch thick)
1 (1 lb. 15 oz.) can pork & beans

2 T. chopped onion
½ tsp. dry mustard
1 (9 oz.) can sliced pineapple
    (drained)

Combine beans, onion, and dry mustard in 1½-quart baking dish. Cut pineapple slices in half. Overlap bacon and pineapple in circle on top of bean mixture. Bake in moderate oven (350°) for 40 minutes. Makes 4 to 5 servings.

ITALIAN SPAGHETTI AND MEATBALLS

MEATBALLS:
1 lb. ground beef	1 beaten egg
⅓ C. fine dry bread crumbs	1 T. water
⅓ C. grated Parmesan cheese	1 T. spaghetti seasoning
¼ tsp. salt	(Presti's)

Mix all ingredients well and form into meatballs. Brown in hot oil and when all are browned, turn heat down and simmer covered until fully cooked.

SPAGHETTI SAUCE:
2 or 3 (15 oz. ea.) cans tomato	2 or 3 T. Presti's spaghetti
sauce	seasoning (Naples style)

Combine, cover and simmer while meatballs are cooking. When meatballs are fully cooked, spoon balls out of grease and into sauce. Add cooked spaghetti and simmer for about 30 minutes.

PORK CHOP CASSEROLE

4 pork chops   1 can cream-style corn

Brown chops and put in casserole; cover with the cream-style corn. Bake at 350° for about 50 minutes or until tender. This is so easy, but so tasty.

LASAGNA

SIMMER FOR 1 HOUR:
½ lb. hamburger   1 tsp. oregano
1 lb. sausage   1 tsp. parsley flakes
½ C. chopped onion   ¼ tsp. chili powder
2 small cans chunk tomatoes or   2 cloves of garlic
   1 lg. & 1 sm. can tomato sauce

Cook 6 lasagna noodles, rinse in cold water; drain. In a medium bowl mix 1 small package cottage cheese, 1 egg (beaten), 1 tsp. parsley flakes, and ½ tsp. salt. In bottom of a 9x13-inch dish, spoon 1 C. sauce and layer 3 noodles. Spread with ½ cottage cheese mixture and top with ½ mozzarella cheese. Spoon on 1 C. sauce over cheese and sprinkle with Parmesan cheese and repeat for 2nd layer. Top with ¾ lb. mozzarella cheese and 3 oz. Parmesan cheese (or to taste). Cover with foil and bake for 25 minutes. Bake, uncovered for 25 minutes at 350°.

LEFTOVER CHEESEY BEEF NOODLE

1 pkg. frozen or dry egg noodles
1 C. beef gravy
1 C. roast beef (chopped)

1 C. Velveeta cheese (cubed)
1 can cream of chicken soup

Cook noodles and drain. Heat gravy and soup together. Add cheese and stir in beef and cooked noodles. Put in a 2-quart casserole. Bake at 350° for 30 minutes.

ROSY BEEF NOODLE CASSEROLE

4 oz. wide noodles
2 T. fat
¾ lb. ground beef
½ C. chopped onion
1 can tomato soup

1¼ C. milk or consomme
1½ tsp. salt
¼ tsp. pepper
½ C. buttered crumbs

Cook noodles, rinse and drain. Heat fat, add beef and onion, cook until lightly browned, stirring frequently. Add soup, milk, and seasonings. Mix sauce and noodles and place in greased casserole. Top with crumbs and bake at 350° for 50 minutes. Makes 6 servings.

SAUSAGE CASSEROLE

Brown 1 lb. sausage and 1 small onion (cut-up) in large skillet. Pour off grease. Add 2 T. flour and stir in. Add enough milk to make a gravy. Add 1 can of cream of mushroom or cream of celery soup. Have cooked and drained ¾ pkg. of noodles. Mix all together in baking dish. Salt and pepper to taste and sprinkle with crushed potato chips or grated cheese on top. Bake at 350° for 30 minutes or until the cheese is thoroughly melted.

CHEESEBURGER PIE

1 pie shell frozen or
   your favorite recipe
1 lb. ground beef
1 tsp. salt
½ tsp. oregano
¼ tsp. pepper

½ C. dry bread crumbs
1 (8 oz.) can tomato sauce
Minced onion, to your taste
1 T. Presti's or
   Italian seasoning

Heat oven to 425°. In medium skillet, cook and stir meat until brown. Drain off fat. Stir in salt, oregano, pepper, crumbs, tomato sauce, onion, and Presti's. Turn into pastry-lined pie pan. Spread cheese topping over filling. Bake for 30 minutes and serve with tomato sauce, if desired.

CHEESE TOPPING:
1 egg
¼ C. milk
½ tsp. salt

½ tsp. dry mustard
½ tsp. Worcestershire sauce
2 C. shredded Cheddar cheese

Beat egg and milk; stir in seasonings and cheese.

HAMBURGER PIE

1 medium onion
1 lb. hamburger
Salt & pepper, to suit taste
1 (No. 2) can French-style beans
   (drained)

1 can tomato soup
5 medium potatoes (cooked)
½ C. warm milk
1 beaten egg

Cook onion and hamburger together. Add drained beans and soup. Pour into 1½-quart casserole. Mash the potatoes and add milk, egg, and seasoning. Spoon over meat. Bake at 350° for 30 minutes.

ITALIAN MEAT PIE

1 lb. ground beef
⅓ C. green pepper (chopped)
¾ C. water
6 oz. can tomato paste
1½ oz. pkg. spaghetti sauce mix

1 deep dish pie crust shell
⅓ C. grated Parmesan cheese
1½ C. grated mozzarella
   cheese

Preheat oven to 400°. Brown ground beef in large skillet; drain. Add green peppers and cook for 2 minutes. Stir in water, tomato paste, and spaghetti sauce mix. Cover and simmer for 10 minutes. Sprinkle half of the Parmesan cheese over bottoms of frozen pie shell. Shread half of meat mixture in pie shell. Sprinkle 1 C. of the mozzarella cheese over meat. Layer remaining meat and Parmesan cheese. Bake on cookie sheet for 16 minutes as it may boil over. Sprinkle top with remaining mozzarella cheese. Return to oven until cheese melts. Serves 6.

EASY HAMBURGER SKILLET

1 lb. hamburger
1 diced onion
1 can tomato soup

1 can Chunky vegetable soup
1 can garbanzo beans

Brown and drain hamburger and onion. Mix remaining ingredients with hamburger and simmer to blend flavors.

SPICY BEEF WEDGES

1 lb. ground beef
¼ C. chopped peppers
½ tsp. chili powder

½ tsp. salt
¼ tsp. pepper
1 (10½ oz.) can pizza sauce

Simmer for 15 to 20 minutes.

CRUST:
1 (8½ oz.) pkg. corn muffin mix

Top with 2 C. mozzarella cheese and bake at 400° for 20 minutes.

SHIP WRECK

LAYER 1:
Sliced raw potatoes

LAYER 4:
Seasoned ground beef

LAYER 2:
Chopped onion

LAYER 5:
Tomato & rice soup

LAYER 3:
10 oz. can pork & beans

Bake at 350° until beef and potatoes are done, about a hour. Take out of the oven and cover with a thin layer of cheese. Return to the oven for 10 or 15 minutes more.

MEALS IN FOIL

6 (18x12-inch) pieces heavy
   duty foil
1½ lb. ground beef
6 large slices onion
1 pkg. brown gravy mix

Salt & pepper
10 oz. pkg. mixed vegetables
   (partially thawed)
1 lb. pkg. frozen tater tots

Divide ground beef into 6 patties. Arrange on foil 1 pattie, onion slice, sprinkle with 2 tsp. gravy mix, salt, and pepper to taste, ⅓ C. vegetables and 7 or 8 potato pieces. Wrap and place on grill or hot campfire for 30 minutes.

"SESAME" MEATBALL DINNER

1 lb. ground beef	2 T. sesame seeds (optional)
1 C. shredded raw potatoes	1 egg (beaten)
1 T. dried parsley flakes	2 C. water
½ tsp. salt	1½ T. instant beef bouillon
¼ tsp. pepper	2 T. cornstarch
1 small onion (chopped fine)	2 T. water

Mix all ingredients, except water, bouillon and cornstarch in medium mixing bowl. Shape into 12 meatballs; set aside. Combine 2 C. water and instant bouillon in 2-quart glass casserole. Cover with lid or plastic wrap. Microwave on High for 6 to 7 minutes until boiling. Add meatballs and recover. Microwave on Roast for 8 minutes. Stir in a mixture of cornstarch and 2 T. water; recover. Microwave on Roast for 3 to 4 minutes until sauce is thickened. Let stand for 5 minutes before serving.

HAMBURGER CASSEROLE

Loosely pack 1 lb. uncooked hamburger in bottom of an 8 or 9-inch square baking pan. Cover with sliced onions then sliced cheese. Top with an undiluted can of soup (celery, mushroom or cream of chicken). Over this, place a layer of frozen tater tots. Don't salt. Bake at 350° for 1 hour.

SEVEN LAYER CASSEROLE

1 C. uncooked rice	½ C. finely chopped onion
1 C. canned or frozen corn	½ C. chopped green pepper
Salt & pepper	¾ lb. uncooked ground beef
2 cans tomato sauce	4 strips bacon (cut-up)
¾ C. water	

Layer ingredients in a 2-quart baking dish with a tight lid as follows: rice, corn, salt, pepper, 1 can tomato sauce, and ½ can water. Next add onion and green pepper, ground beef, salt, pepper, and a second can of tomato sauce with ¼ C. water. Cover meat with bacon. Cover and bake at 350° for 1 hour. Uncover, and bake for about 30 minutes longer until bacon is crispy. Serves 4 to 6.

PIZZA LOAF

1 (1 lb.) loaf frozen bread dough (thawed)
1 lb. ground pork or ground beef
¼ C. mushrooms (optional)
½ C. diced onion
1 tsp. salt
¼ tsp. pepper

1 (8 oz.) can tomato sauce
1 tsp. paprika
½ tsp. oregano
½ tsp. garlic salt
¼ lb. Cheddar cheese
¾ C. mozzarella cheese
2 T. melted margarine

Let loaf of thawed dough rise, following label directions. Prepare filling by cooking meat, onion, salt, and pepper til no pink remains. Drain off fat. Stir in tomato sauce and spices. Bring to boil and lower heat, cover, and simmer for 30 minutes or less. Cool mixture. Punch down dough. Roll out on floured surface to 15 x 12-inch rectangle. Lift dough onto greased cookie sheet. Spoon meat filling down center third of dough. Sprinkle with cheeses. Make diagonal cuts in dough 1½-inch apart, down each side, cutting to within ½-inch of filling. Criss-cross strips of dough over filling, pressing down and sealing with a drop of water. Brush top of loaf with melted oleo. Bake at 350° for 30 minutes. Cut in thick slices to serve.

SKILLET CASSEROLE

1 lb. ground beef
1 lb. ground pork sausage
½ lb. longhorn cheese
1 onion
1 green pepper

½ lb. noodles
Salt, to taste
1 can tomato soup
1 can water
1 can mushrooms

Brown meat, onion, and green pepper in skillet. Add everything but the cheese and cook for 15 minutes or until noodles are done. Put in casserole and sprinkle with crumbled cheese; cook in oven at 350° for 30 to 45 minutes or until cheese is melted.

68

STEAK CASSEROLE

Brown favorite steak in skillet with seasonings and place in big casserole or roaster. Mix the following and pour over steak:

1 C. uncooked elbow macaroni	4 or 5 large sliced carrots
½ C. rice (not cooked)	1 C. catsup
1 big onion (sliced)	Enough hot water to cover

Bake at 350° for 1 hour or until carrots are done.

SKILLET HASH

2 C. chopped cooked beef	⅔ C. chopped onion
2 C. chopped cooked potatoes	2 T. chopped parsley
Dash of salt & pepper	(if desired)
¼ C. shortening	⅔ C. water

Combine beef, potatoes, onion, parsley, salt, and pepper. Melt shortening in large skillet over medium heat. Spread mixture in skillet. Brown hash 10 to 15 minutes, turning frequently with a wide spatula. Stir in water. Reduce heat, cover and cook for 10 minutes or until crisp.

SHIRLEY'S BEANS

1 lb. hamburger (brown & drain)	½ C. catsup
1 large onion	2 lbs. vinegar
½ lb. bacon (brown & drain)	1 tsp. mustard
1 can red beans	¾ C. brown sugar
1 can green lima beans	½ C. white sugar
1 can pork & beans (1 lb. 5 oz.)	

Bake at 375°, uncovered for 1 hour and 15 minutes or crock pot for ½ day.

FARMERS CASSEROLE

1 lb. hamburger	1 C. water
3 T. oil	2 tsp. salt
½ C. chopped onioni	¼ tsp. pepper
¼ C. diced celery	2 tsp. parsley
1 tsp. minced garlic	1 tsp. oregano
1 can tomato paste	2 C. grated Cheddar cheese
1 (8 oz.) can tomato sauce	1 C. grated Mozzarella cheese
1 lb. can tomatoes	1 pkg. rigatoni noodles

Combine the first 5 ingredients in skillet and brown. Add tomatoes, paste, and sauce; water, salt, pepper, parsley, and oregano. Simmer for 1 hour. Add cheeses. Combined with 1 pkg. rigatoni noodles - cooked as directed, drained and rinsed with cold water. Bake in casserole dish for 1 hour at 325°.

MASHED BROWN OMELET

4 slices bacon	¼ C. milk
2 C. shredded potatoes	4 eggs
¼ C. chopped onion	1 C. shredded cheese
¼ C. green pepper	

In a 10 or 12-inch skillet cook bacon till crisp. Leave drippings in skillet and drain bacon and crumble. Mix next 3 ingredients and put into skillet. Cook over low heat till crisp and brown. Blend eggs, milk, salt, and a dash of pepper; pour over potatoes. Top with cheese and bacon; cover. Cook over low heat for 10 minutes. Serve in wedges. Serves 4. (Dot's note - this makes a delicious Sunday evening supper.)

GRANDMA'S SOUP HOT DISH

1½ C. diced raw potatoes (4 medium-sized)	1 lb. hamburger
	1 C. minestrone soup
Meatballs (made like meat loaf)	1 C. cream of mushroom soup
½ C. water	

No seasoning. Put in Dutch oven for 1½ hours.

HAMBURGER CASSEROLE

Cook 1 lb. hamburger and chopped onions until brown.

ADD:

2 C. dry noodles	1 can cream of celery or
1 C. carrots	mushroom soup
1 C. chopped cabbage	1 can vegetable soup
1 small can tomato sauce	

Bake at 325° for 1 hour.

MANICOTTI DISH

1 lb. hamburge˙ or sausage	1 egg
1 large onion (chopped)	Salt & pepper
1 clove garlic (chopped)	1 pkg. manicotti
8 oz. mozzarella cheese (shredded)	2 jars (15½ oz. ea.) spaghetti
½ C. bread crumbs	sauce
¼ C. chopped parsley	⅓ C. dry red wine
	½ C. grated Parmesan cheese

In a skillet, brown meat, onion, and garlic. Drain excess fat and cool. Stir in cheese, crumbs, parsley, and eggs. Season to taste with salt and pepper. Cook shells in boiling salted water until tender (15 minutes); drain. Use meat mixture to stuff shells. Spoon ½ of sauce in bottom of a 9x13-inch pan. Place shells on top of sauce, side by side in a single layer. Mix wine with remaining sauce and pour over shells. Sprinkle with cheese. Bake in a preheated hot oven (400°) for 20 to 25 minutes until brown and bubbly. Serve sprinkled with additional grated Parmesan cheese.

ELBOW CASSEROLE

½ lb. ground beef
½ C. chopped onion
1 (1 lb.) can tomatoes (cut-up)
¾ tsp. salt
1/8 tsp. pepper

1/8 tsp. cinnamon
½ C. grated Parmesan cheese
1 (8 oz.) box elbow macaroni
(cooked & drained)
3 T. butter or margarine

Cook beef and onion until brown and onion is tender. Add tomatoes, ½ tsp. salt, the pepper, and cinnamon; simmer for 15 minutes. Stir in ¼ C. cheese and cooked macaroni. Turn into 12x8x2-inch baking dish; set aside. In medium sauce pan, melt butter, blend in flour and remaining ¼ tsp. salt. Gradually stir in milk and cook; stir until sauce thickens. About 5 minutes. Cool slightly. Beat in eggs, 1 at a time. Stir in remaining ¼ C. cheese and pour over meat mixture. Place in preheated 400° oven; lower temperature to 375° and bake at 30 to 40 minutes or until top is golden brown and knife inserted in center comes out clean. Makes 6 to 8 servings. Note: Casserole can be frozen after baking.

HASH

1½ lbs. hamburger
¾ C. uncooked rice
1 T. chili powder
4 C. tomatoes

1 tsp. salt
½ tsp. pepper
Chopped onion (optional)
2 T. green pepper (optional)

Brown the hamburger, onion, and peppers; drain the grease. Combine all ingredients and place in greased 2-quart casserole. Cover and put in oven at 350° for 50 to 60 minutes.

COOKIES

TRI-LEVEL BROWNIES

1 C. quick cooking rolled oats
½ C. flour
½ C. packed brown sugar
¼ tsp. baking soda
6 T. butter (melted)
¾ C. sugar
¼ C. butter (melted)
1 (1 oz.) sq. unsweetened chocolate (melted & cooled)

1 egg
⅔ C. flour
¼ tsp. baking powder
¼ C. milk
¼ tsp. vanilla
½ C. walnuts, chopped
Fudge frosting

For Bottom Layer: Stir together first 4 ingredients and ¼ tsp. salt. Stir in 6 T. melted butter. Pat in 11x7½x1½-inch baking pan. Bake at 350° for 10 minutes.

For Middle Layer: Combine sugar, ¼ C. butter, and chocolate; add egg. Beat well. Stir in ⅔ C. flour, baking powder, and ¼ tsp. salt. Add to chocolate mixture alternately with a mixture of milk and vanilla, mixing after each addition. Fold in nuts. Spread batter over baked layer. Continue baking at 350° for 25 minutes. Cool and frost with Fudge Frosting. Top with walnut halves.

FUDGE FROSTING:
In small saucepan, melt 1 (1 oz.) sq. unsweetened chocolate and 2 T. butter over low heat; stirring constantly. Remove from heat and stir in 1½ C. powdered sugar (sifted) and 1 tsp. vanilla. Blend in hot water, about 2 T. to make almost pourable consistency.

OATMEAL BROWNIES

1 C. oleo	1½ tsp. salt
¾ C. cocoa	1½ tsp. baking powder
2⅔ C. sugar	1½ C. dry oatmeal
4 eggs	2 tsp. vanilla
1 C. flour	Nuts (optional)
½ C. wheat germ	

Mix first 4 ingredients. Add other ingredients. Bake in a 10x15-inch jelly roll pan at 350° for 20 to 25 minutes.

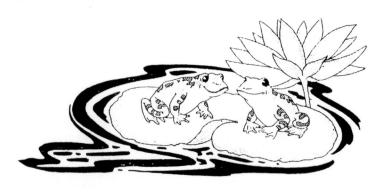

BROWNIES

1½ C. flour	1½ C. sugar
1 tsp. baking powder	3 eggs
½ tsp. salt	1 tsp. vanilla
½ tsp. cinnamon	1 C. crushed pineapple
¾ C. butter or oleo	2 sq. chocolate
	½ C. chopped nuts

Sift dry ingredients, cream butter and sugar, add eggs, beating until light; add vanilla and dry ingredients. Put 1 C. of dough in second bowl and add pineapple. To dough in first bowl add 2 sqs. of chocolate and nuts. Spread 1½ C. chocolate dough in 13x9x2-inch pan. Cover with white mixture, drop chocolate dough by spoonful on white mixture, drop chocolate dough by spoonful on white dough and spread. Bake at 350° for 45 minutes. Frost with chocolate frosting.

MARSHMELLOW BROWNIES

1 C. butterscotch chips   ½ C. butter

Melt in 3-quart saucepan over medium heat, stirring constantly. Remove from heat and cool to lukewarm.

1½ C. flour   ½ tsp. salt
⅔ C. brown sugar   1 tsp. vanilla
2 tsp. baking powder   2 eggs

Mix well and add to first mixture.

2 C. miniature marshmallows   ½ C. nuts
1 C. chocolate chips

Mix and fold into above mixture just until combined - 5 strokes. Bake at 350° for 20 to 25 minutes in 9x13-inch pan. Center will be jiggily but firms when cool. Don't overbake.

NUTTY PUDDING BARS

1 (12 oz.) pkg. semi-sweet
  chocolate chips
1 (12 oz.) pkg. butterscotch chips
1 (12 oz.) jar peanut butter
1 oz. unsweetened chocolate
1 C. butter or margarine
2½ C. coarsely chopped peanuts

½ of 1 (4-serving) size pkg.
  (5 T.) reg. vanilla
  pudding mix
⅓ C. evaporated milk
1 tsp. vanilla
2 lbs. powdered sugar

Combine chocolate and butterscotch chips, peanut butter, and unsweetened chocolate. Stir over low heat until melted. Spread half of mixture in 15x10x1-inch pan and chill until set. Let remaining mixture stand, covered at room temperature. Combine butter, pudding mix, and milk. Cook and stir to melt butter; stir in vanilla. Turn into large mixer bowl and beat in sugar till smooth. Spread over chilled layer and sprinkle with nuts. Spread remaining chocolate over all and chill till firm.

PEANUT BUSTER PARFAIT BARS

1 pkg. crushed Oreos
3 C. powdered sugar
2 sticks oleo
4 eggs

3 sq. semi-sweet chocolate
½ gallon softened vanilla ice
  cream
1 C. salted peanuts

Put all but ½ C. Oreos in bottom of a 9x13-inch pan. Cook oleo, eggs, powdered sugar, and chocolate in pan; bring to a rolling boil. Add peanuts and spread over Oreos. Let cool and spread ice cream over cooked layer. Top with remaining Oreos. Store in freezer.

COOKIES

1¾ C. sifted flour   ½ tsp. soda
½ tsp. salt

Mix the above ingredients into 1 C. sugar and 1 tsp. vanilla.

ADD:
1 egg (unbeaten)   ½ C. oleo, melted with
                                          2 sq. chocolate

ADD:
½ C. sour milk   ½ C. nuts

Drop by teaspoon on greased cookie sheet. Bake at 400° for 10 to 12 minutes.
Frost with chocolate frosting. (To sour milk use 1 T. vinegar to ½ C. milk.)

FRUIT PUNCH BARS

2 eggs   1½ tsp. soda
1½ C. sugar   ½ tsp. salt
1 lb. 1 oz. can fruit cocktail   1 tsp. vanilla
   (undrained)   1⅓ C. coconut
2¼ C. flour   ½ C. chopped nuts

Grease and flour 15x10-inch pan. Beat eggs and sugar at high speed of the
mixer until light and fluffy. Add fruit cocktail, flour, soda, salt, and vanilla.
Beat at medium speed until well blended. Spread in pan and sprinkle with
coconut and nuts. Bake at 350° for 20 to 25 minutes or until golden brown.
While hot drizzle with the following glaze. Cool and cut into bars.

GLAZE:
¾ C. sugar   ½ tsp. vanilla
½ C. butter   ½ C. chopped nuts
¼ C. evaporated milk

Combine all ingredients, except nuts. Boil for 2 minutes, stirring constantly.
Remove from heat and stir in nuts; cool.

PUMPKIN BARS

4 eggs
1 C. salad oil

2 C. sugar
1 C. pumpkin

Mix well and add the following:

1 tsp. soda
1 tsp. baking powder
½ tsp. salt

2 tsp. cinnamon
2 C. flour
1 C. nuts

Stir and pour in 9x13-inch pan. Bake at 350° for 20 minutes and cool.

FROSTING:
3 oz. cream cheese
6 T. butter or oleo

3 C. powdered sugar
1 tsp. vanilla

Add milk to make spreadable consistency. (Dorothia uses 2 C. of pumpkin and Marcia uses ¾ C. melted margarine instead of oil.)

THREE-LAYER COOKIES

1 C. shortening
½ C. white sugar
½ C. brown sugar
2 slightly beaten egg yolks
1 tsp. cold water

1 tsp. vanilla
2 C. flour
¼ tsp. salt
1 tsp. baking powder
¼ tsp. soda

Thoroughly cream shortening; gradually add white and brown sugars. Add egg yolks, water, and vanilla; mix together. Sift dry ingredients and add to the creamed mixture. Spread evenly in greased 9x13-inch pan and pat down with your hand. Sprinkle 1 (6 oz.) pkg. chocolate chips evenly over the first layer and press down lightly. Mix 1 C. brown sugar and 2 beaten egg whites. Beat egg whites until stiff and gradually add brown sugar. Spread over the second layer. Bake at 375° for 25 minutes. Cool and cut into squares. Let stand for 4 hours before serving.

BUTTERSCOTCH CHIP COOKIES

1 C. brown sugar
1 C. white sugar
1 C. oleo
1 C. Wesson Oil
1 egg
1 tsp. vanilla
1 C. oatmeal

3 C. flour
1 C. Rice Krispies
½ tsp. salt
1 tsp. soda
1 C. coconut
½ C. nuts
1 pkg. (12 oz.) butterscotch chips

Bake at 350° for 10 to 12 minutes. Leave on cookie sheet a few minutes to set.

CHOCOLATE OATMEAL COOKIES

1 C. flour
1 tsp. baking powder
½ tsp. salt
½ C. butter
1 C. sugar
1 egg (beaten)

2 sq. chocolate (melted)
½ tsp. vanilla
½ tsp. almond extract
1 C. quick oatmeal
½ C. nuts

Sift together flour, baking powder, and salt. Cream butter and sugar; beat in egg, chocolate, and flavorings. Mix in flour and stir in oatmeal and nuts. Drop by teaspoonful on baking sheets and flatten with a knife dipped in water. Bake for 8 to 10 minutes in 350° oven.

CHOCOLATE COOKIES

1½ C. oleo
2 C. white sugar
1 C. brown sugar
3 eggs
1 T. vanilla

5¼ C. flour
1 tsp. soda
1 tsp. salt
5 T. cocoa
1 C. sour milk

Cream first 5 ingredients. Sift dry ingredients and mix with your first mixture and milk. (1 C. of nuts are optional.) Bake at 350° for 10 to 12 minutes. Frost with frosting.

MOLASSES COOKIES

1 C. shortening (lard is excellent)
1 C. sugar
1 C. sorghum
1 egg (well-beaten)
2 tsp. soda

1 tsp. ginger
2 tsp. cinnamon
½ C. cold water
Flour to make stiff dough,
    about 4½ C.

Roll out and cut with cookie cutter. Sprinkle crushed peppermint stick candy on top before baking. Bake at 375°.

OATMEAL ICE BOX COOKIES

1 C. fat (oleo preferred)
1 C. white sugar
1 C. brown sugar
2 eggs
1 tsp. vanilla
½ C. dates (finely chopped or ground)

1½ C. flour
3 C. oatmeal
1 tsp. soda
1 tsp. baking powder
½ C. nuts (optional)

Cream butter and sugar; add eggs and vanilla. Mix flour, salt, baking powder, and soda; add to the first mixture, then add oatmeal, nuts, and chopped dates. Shape into a roll. Wrap in waxed paper and chill overnight or a portion stored in the freezer for a time if you don't want so many. When ready to bake, slice, and bake at 350° till nicely browned. They may be frosted, if desired.

FROSTING:
3 T. butter
1 C. powdered sugar
½ tsp. cinnamon

1 T. strong coffee
1 tsp. vanilla

OATMEAL SUGAR COOKIES

1 C. sugar
1 C. brown sugar
2 sticks oleo
2 eggs
½ tsp. salt
½ tsp. baking powder

1 tsp. soda
1 tsp. cinnamon
3 C. old-fashioned oatmeal
1½ C. flour
1 tsp. vanilla
1 C. raisins (optional)

Cream sugars and shortening; add eggs. Sift baking powder, soda, salt, cinnamon, and flour together. Add to creamed mixture; add oatmeal and vanilla. Drop by teaspoons into sugar. Bake on greased cookie sheet at 350° for about 8 minutes. Makes about 50 cookies.

BUTTERSCOTCH QUICKIES

Melt 1 (12 oz.) pkg. butterscotch chips and ½ C. peanut butter. Remove from heat and add the following:

2 C. cornflakes   1 C. flaked coconut

Drop by teaspoon onto waxed paper lined cookie sheet and chill.

SPRITZ COOKIES

1½ C. oleo   1 tsp. vanilla
1½ C. brown sugar   1 tsp. cream of tartar
1½ C. sugar   1 tsp. soda
2 eggs (beaten)   5 C. of flour (or a little more)

Cream oleo and sugars. Add eggs and sifted dry ingredients and vanilla. Add flour to make a firm dough. Press through cookie maker and bake for 8 to 10 minutes or until very lightly browned at 375°.

SUGAR COOKIES

1 C. granulated sugar   2 tsp. vanilla
1 C. powdered sugar   1 tsp. cream of tartar
1 C. margarine   1 tsp. soda
1 C. oil   5¼ C. flour
2 beaten eggs

Cream sugars with margarine and add eggs. Stir in oil and vanilla. Mix dry ingredients and blend in. Refrigerate overnight. Form into balls and dip in granulated sugar and flatten with bottom of glass. Bake at 350° until lightly browned. I sometimes use brown sugar instead of granulated. May use part almond or other flavoring. Substitute 2 C. quick oatmeal for part of flour. Add chocolate chips or caraway seed or chopped dates, nuts, etc.

PEANUT BUTTER OATMEAL COOKIES

1 C. white sugar
1 C. brown sugar
1 C. shortening
2 eggs
1 tsp. vanilla flavoring
½ tsp. butterscotch flavoring

½ tsp. butter flavoring
1 C. peanut butter
2 C. flour
1 tsp. baking powder
1 tsp. soda
1 C. bran flakes
1 C. quick-cooking rolled oats

Cream the sugars with the shortening. Beat in eggs. Add the flavorings and peanut butter. Sift the flour, baking powder, and soda together; mix into creamed mixture. Fold in the bran flakes and rolled oats. Drop by teaspoonfuls onto ungreased baking sheet. Bake at 350° for 8 to 10 minutes. May press down with fork if you like.

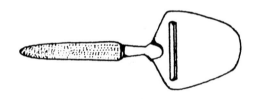

FRUIT COCKTAIL COOKIES

1 C. white sugar
1 C. brown sugar
1 C. shortening
3 eggs
2 C. fruit cocktail (well-drained)
1 C. raisins
½ C. nutmeats

4 C. flour
1 tsp. baking powder
1 tsp. soda
1 tsp. nutmeg
1 tsp. cinnamon
½ tsp. salt
1 tsp. vanilla

Cream sugars and shortening. Add eggs, then flour, soda, baking powder, nutmeg, cinnamon, salt, and vanilla; mix well. Add fruit cocktail, raisins, and nutmeats. Drop by tablespoons full onto cookie sheet. Bake in 350° to 375° oven.

THREE LAYER NO-BAKE COOKIES
(This is a bar type cookie)

⅓ C. butter
¼ C. sugar
¼ C. cocoa
1 tsp. vanilla

1 egg (slightly beaten)
1 C. flaked coconut
2 C. graham cracker crumbs
½ C. chopped nuts

Place butter, sugar, cocoa, and vanilla in double boiler. Cook until blended. Add egg and cook for 5 minutes longer, stirring constantly. Add coconut, cracker crumbs, and nuts. Press into 8x12-inch pan. Cool.

¼ C. oleo
3 T. milk

2 C. powdered sugar
2 tsp. instant vanilla
pudding mix

Cream oleo and milk with pudding mix; add to oleo. Add sugar and beat until smooth. Spread on first layer and chill. Melt ¾ C. chocolate chips and spread over top. Store in refrigerator.

FRUIT CAKE COOKIES

1 C. shortening
2 C. brown sugar
4 C. flour
1 tsp. baking soda
1 tsp. salt
2 eggs

⅔ C. sour milk
1 C. English walnuts (chopped)
1 jar maraschino cherries
(cut-up)
1 box (2 C.) mixed candied
fruit
2 C. chopped dates

Cream shortening and sugar; add eggs and sour milk. Stir in mixed dry ingredients; add nuts, cherries, fruit, and dates. This is a colorful Christmas cookie. Chill dough several hours and bake on lightly greased pan at 350° for 12 minutes or if you have the small gem pans, you can use them.

DESSERTS

Strawberry Dessert

CAKE:

4 eggs (separated)
¼ tsp. salt
2 tsp. vanilla

⅓ C. sugar
⅔ C. all-purpose flour

Grease a 10x15x1-inch pan. Cover with foil and grease foil. Beat together egg whites and salt until the mixture forms stiff peaks. Beat vanilla and egg yolks together. Fold in about ½ C. of the beaten egg whites. Fold in remaining whites with flour. Spread evenly into pan. Bake at 400° for 10 to 12 minutes. Loosen around the edges and turn it out onto a powdered-sugared towel. Roll up and leave the cake until cool. Unfold and spread on filling.

FILLING:

1½ C. berries (any type)
1 C. heavy whipping cream

2 T. powdered sugar
2 tsp. vanilla

Combine cream, sugar, and vanilla. Mix until stiff. Fold in berries. Spread mixture evenly over cooled sponge cake. Roll-up like a jelly roll. Sprinkle with powdered sugar. Store in refrigerator.

Pumpkin Cake Roll

3 eggs
1 C. sugar
⅔ C. pumpkin (½ of 15 oz. can)
1 tsp. lemon juice
¾ C. flour
1 tsp. ginger
½ tsp. nutmeg

½ tsp. salt
2 tsp. cinnamon
1 C. finely chopped walnuts
1 C. powdered sugar
2 (3 oz. ea.) pkgs. cream cheese
4 T. butter
1 tsp. vanilla

Beat eggs for 5 minutes. Gradually beat in sugar; stir in pumpkin and lemon juice. Stir together flour, ginger, nutmeg, salt, and cinnamon. Fold into pumpkin mixture. Spread into greased and floured 10x15x1-inch pan. Top with walnuts. Bake at 375° for 15 minutes. Turn out on flour sack towel. Sprinkle with powdered sugar. Starting at narrow end; roll towel and cake together. Cool and carefully unroll. Combine powdered sugar, cream cheese, butter, and vanilla. Beat until smooth. Spread over cake and roll back up. Wrap in foil, freeze or refrigerate. If frozen put in refrigerator for 2 hours before cutting. For best serving results, cut with electric knife, approximately pinwheel width, to stretch. Cut pinwheels in half.

FOUR LAYER DESSERT

1 stick oleo   A pinch of salt
1 C. flour

Mix and press this into a 9x13-inch pan. Bake at 350° for 15 minutes. Then let cool.

SECOND LAYER:
1 pkg. Dream Whip (prepared)   1/8 oz. cream cheese
1 C. powdered sugar

Mix and put on first layer.

THIRD LAYER:
2 boxes instant lemon pudding   3 C. milk

Spread this on top of second layer.

FOURTH LAYER:
1 pkg. Dream Whip (prepared)

Spread on top of third layer.

Apple Crisp

1 (1 lb. 6 oz.) can apple pie filling
Brown sugar
½ tsp. cinnamon
¼ tsp. nutmeg

2 T. lemon juice
½ pkg. white cake mix
¾ stick butter

Pour apples into a 9-inch pie pan. Sprinkle lightly with brown sugar, cinnamon, nutmeg, and lemon juice. Cover apples with cake mix, completely cover cake mix with thinly sliced pats of butter. Bake at 350° until top is browned and bubbling, about 45 minutes. Serve warm with whipped cream. Serves 6 to 8.

Snowy Pears Helene

1 can pear halves (chilled)
Cool Whip

Chocolate sauce

Drain the chilled can of pears. Place pears in individual serving dishes, cut side up. Top each with generous spoonful of Cool Whip. Drizzle with a chocolate sauce. Makes 4 to 6 servings.

Easy Cherry Dessert

1 can sweetened cond. milk
1 large pkg. cream cheese
1 large can crushed drained pineapple

1 large can cherry pie filling
Graham cracker crust

Mix milk and cream cheese; stir in pineapple and cherry filling. Blend with mixer. Pour over graham cracker crust. Use 9x13-inch pan or 2 pie pans. Can make own crust. Can be served at once, but best if cold. Can be used as salad, if desired or without crust, but is very rich.

Chocolate Forever

6 eggs (separated)
1 C. sugar
1 tsp. vanilla
40 Ritz crackers
½ C. sugar
½ C. cocoa

2 C. powdered sugar
½ C. butter
2 eggs
½ tsp. vanilla
Cool Whip
Hershey bar

Beat 6 egg whites to soft peak. Gradually add 1 C. sugar. Beat until stiff. Add 1 tsp. vanilla. Crush 40 Ritz crackers and combine with ½ C. sugar. Fold in egg whites. Spread in buttered 9x13-inch pan. Bake at 350° for 30 minutes. Cool. Combine cocoa, powdered sugar, butter, eggs, and vanilla. Beat well, at least 5 minutes. Spread over crust. Cover with Cool Whip. Top with shredded Hershey bar. Keep refrigerated.

ICE CREAM CAKE ROLL

4 egg yolks
¼ C. sugar

½ tsp. vanilla

Beat egg yolks until thick and lemon colored, gradually beat in the ½ C. sugar and vanilla.

4 egg whites

½ C. sugar

Beat egg whites until almost stiff, gradually add the ½ C. sugar and beat until very stiff.

¾ C. cake flour (if you don't
  have cake flour, put 1 T.
  cornstarch in each cup of flour)

1 tsp. baking powder
¼ tsp. salt

Fold yolks into whites. Sift or mix together dry ingredients and add to egg mixture. Fold in. Bake in greased, waxed paper lined 15½x10½-inch pan or cookie sheet at 375° for 12 minutes. Sprinkle powdered sugar on towel. Put cake upside down on towel, remove wax paper, roll up the cake with the towel. When cool put ice cream between and roll and freeze.

Easy Apple Crisp

½ C. butter
½ C. brown sugar
½ C. white sugar
¾ C. flour

4 C. diced apples
2 T. water
2 tsp. cinnamon
½ C. oatmeal

Mix cinnamon, butter, sugars, flour, and oatmeal. Pour over apples in 8x8-inch pan. Bake at 350° for 1 hour. Can easily double this recipe and use double ingredients and 9x13-inch pan.

Heath Bar Yummie

12 graham crackers (crushed)
12 soda crackers (crushed)
1 stick (½ C.) margarine (softened)
2 (3¾ oz. ea.) pkgs. vanilla instant pudding mix

2 C. cold milk
1 qt. softened vanilla ice cream
1 carton Cool Whip
2 frozen Heath or Butterfinger candy bars

Mix graham crackers, soda crackers, and margarine. Put ⅔ of crumbs in a 9x13-inch pan. Beat pudding mix and milk. Add ice cream and mix well. Pour over crumbs in pan and chill until firm. Spread Cool Whip over top. Crush candy bars and mix with remaining crumbs. Sprinkle on top of Cool Whip. Chill. Also good using chocolate pudding and chocolate ice cream.

Lemon Sponge Mini Cakes

2 T. butter	Pinch of salt
1 C. sugar	5 T. lemon juice
3 eggs (separated)	Grated rind of 1 lemon
1½ C. milk	4 T. all-purpose flour

Cream butter. Add sugar, all-purpose flour, salt, lemon juice, and rind of 1 lemon. Stir in beaten egg yolks, mixed with milk. Fold in stiffly beaten egg whites. Pour into custard cups. Set the cups in a pan of hot water and bake about 40 minutes in a moderate oven. When done each cup will contain custard at the bottom and sponge cake on top. (Will fill 6 or 7 custard cups.) Serve hot or chilled.

FROZEN DESSERT

2 C. vanilla wafer crumbs	1 T. grated lime peel
1 T. cinnamon	6 egg whites
¼ C. butter (softened)	¼ tsp. cream of tartar
6 egg yolks	2 C. whipping cream (whipped)
1 C. sugar	8 drops green food coloring
⅓ C. lime juice	

Combine wafer crumbs, cinnamon, and butter. Press half of mixture in bottom of 9-inch oblong pan; set aside the remainder. Combine egg yolks, ¾ C. sugar, lime juice, and peel. Cook, stirring constantly until thickened; cool. Beat egg whites and cream of tartar until soft peaks form; gradually add remaining ¼ C. sugar, beating until stiff peaks form. Fold into lime mixture; fold in whipped cream and food color. Pour half of mi xture in prepared pan; sprinkle with remaining crumbs. Pour remaining lime filling over crumb layer. Freeze overnight or until firm. Makes 12 servings.

VARIATION: You can use graham crackers instead of vanilla wafer crumbs; lemon juice instead of lime; lemon peel instead of lime; and yellow food coloring instead of green.

Sawlogs

4 eggs (separated)
¾ C. sugar
½ C. sifted all-purpose flour
1 tsp. vanilla

¼ tsp. salt
¼ C. cocoa
¾ tsp. baking powder
Ice cream

Beat egg yolks until fluffy. Add sugar and vanilla; beat. Add sifted dry ingredients and beat until smooth. Whip egg whites and salt until very stiff. Fold into above mixture. Line jelly roll pan with greased brown paper bag. Pour batter on and bake at 375° for 15 minutes. Turn at once onto a towel sprinkled with powdered sugar. Roll up and cool. When cool, unroll. Spread with ¼ gallon softened ice cream. Roll up and freeze. Slice when ready to serve.

RAISIN PUDDING WITH SELF-SAUCE

1 C. flour
½ C. sugar
1 tsp. baking powder
¼ tsp. salt
2 T. shortening
1 egg (beaten)

⅓ C. milk
1 C. raisins
1 C. brown sugar
1 T. oleo
2 C. boiling water

Measure and sift dry ingredients. Cut in shortening as for biscuits. Mix egg and milk; stir into dry mixture with the raisins. Pour into well-greased, deep pan - at least a 2-quart one. Mix remaining ingredients and pour over batter. Bake until batter has come to top and is done in center. Serves 6. Bake at 350°. Sauce will be thin.

SUET PUDDING
(An Old Fashioned Recipe)

1 C. sour milk	1 C. suet (ground fat)
1 tsp. baking soda	2 tsp. cinnamon
1 C. sugar	½ tsp. cloves & allspice
1 C. raisins	

Mix all together using enough flour to make stiff batter. Place in thin cloth. Tie shut leaving enough room to raise. Place on dish in large pan with 1 inch of water. Steam slowly for 2½ hours. Serve warm with sauce.

SAUCE:
¾ C. sugar	2 C. milk
3 T. flour	

Combine and cook till thick. Sprinkle with nutmeg.

CUSTARD BREAD PUDDING

2 eggs	2 C. milk
½ C. sugar	2 slices bread
Dash of salt	½ C. raisins
1 tsp. vanilla	

Beat eggs and add sugar, salt, and milk. Break bread in pieces. Add to mixture and also raisins. Sprinkle with nutmeg. Bake at 350° for 1 hour. Serve with chocolate syrup.

BAKED CUSTARD

¼ C. sugar
2 eggs
Dash of salt

2 C. skim milk
½ tsp. vanilla

Beat eggs slightly. Add sugar and salt. Scald milk until film forms on top. Stir into egg mixture gradually. Add vanilla and put in a baking dish. Set dish in pan of hot water 1-inch deep. Sprinkle nutmeg on top. Bake at 350° for 40 to 50 minutes, just until a knife inserted in center comes out clean. Serve cool or chilled. Only 95 calories per serving.

DATE PUDDING

Mix and place in a 9x9-inch pan:

1 C. sugar
½ C. milk
1 C. dates (chopped)
½ C. nuts

1 C. flour
2 tsp. baking powder
1 tsp. vanilla

Pour over top of batter and heat to boiling:

2 T. butter
2 C. boiling water

Pinch of salt
1 C. brown sugar

Bake at 350° for 40 minutes. Serve with whipped cream or ice cream.

ORANGE MILLS SHERBET

1 C. sugar
1 C. orange juice
2 T. lemon juice

1½ C. milk
½ tsp. salt

Mix sugar with juices and salt. Let stand for 10 minutes. Slowly add milk, stirring constantly. Pour into tray and freeze, stirring at 30 minute intervals for about 2 hours. In about 4 hours, the sherbet will be ready to serve.

ICE CREAM DESSERT

1½ C. crushed Ritz or white
  crackers

7 T. oleo
4 T. sugar

Put above in a 9x13-inch pan. Mix 2 quarts of soft vanilla ice cream and 1 qt. orange sherbet together and place on crumbs. Freeze (Blue Bunny ice cream can be bought already mixed).

SAUCE:
4 T. Realemon
1 C. sugar

6 T. oleo

Cook this until boiling and then add two beaten eggs. Stir and cook until saucey. Cool and pour over ice cream and refreeze.

98

TOFFEE TREAT

1 pkg. saltine crackers
 (10 or 12 doubles)
1 pkg. graham crackers
½ C. margarine
2 pkgs. instant vanilla pudding

6 Heath candy bars*
2 C. milk
1 qt. vanilla ice cream
 (softened)
Pecans
Cool Whip

Roll crackers and mix with melted butter. Put into 9x13-inch pan. Prepare pudding and fold in ice cream and pecans. Pour over crumb mixture. Spread Cool Whip evenly over the filling. Crush the bars and sprinkle over the Cool Whip; refrigerate.

Real Good Bread Pudding

4 C. soft bread (in cubes)
2 C. milk
3 eggs
1 tsp. vanilla

½ tsp. salt
½ C. granulated sugar
Raisins (optional)

Beat eggs; add milk, vanilla, salt, and sugar. Mix together. Add raisins, if desired. Mix with bread cubes and put in greased 8x8-inch pan or 9x9-inch pan. Sprinkle with cinnamon and nutmeg. Bake at 350° to 375° until raised and browned.

NOTE: More bread and milk can be added.

Cheesecake

3 (8 oz. ea.) pkgs. cream cheese (softened)
4 large eggs

1 C. sugar
1 tsp. vanilla

TOPPING:
½ C. sugar
1 C. sour cream

1 tsp. vanilla

Heat oven to 350°. Grease an 8-inch springform pan. In large bowl, with electric mixer, beat cream cheese until smooth and fluffy. Beat in eggs, 1 at a time, then beat in 1 C. sugar and 1 tsp. vanilla. Pour into greased pan. Bake cheesecake for 45 minutes. Remove to wire rack (leave in cake pan); let cool for 25 minutes. Leave oven on. In small bowl, combine 1 C. sour cream, ½ C. sugar, and 1 tsp. vanilla. Spread over top of cheesecake and bake for 15 minutes longer or until mixture is just set. Cool chesecake to room temperature; refrigerate for several hours until well chilled before cutting.

APPLE SLICES

2 C. flour
½ tsp. salt
1 C. shortening
2 egg yolks
1 T. lemon juice
7 or 8 T. water
8 apples

1 C. sugar
1 T. flour
½ tsp. salt
1½ tsp. cinnamon
1 C. powdered sugar
Piece of butter
Warm milk

Combine flour, ½ tsp. salt, shortening, and blend as for pie. In other bowl, beat 2 egg yolks, lemon juice, and water. Add flour mixture and work into ball. Divide in half. Roll out 1 piece to fit 15 x 9-inch pan.

For Filling: Pare, grate, and slice thin the 8 apples. Mix with sugar, flour, salt, and cinnamon. Put mixture on bottom crust. Cover with top crust and prick with fork. After slices are baked, while still warm, brush with icing.

For Icing: Mix well the powdered sugar, piece of butter, and enough warm milk for a thin consistency.

BUSTER BAR DESSERT

2 C. powdered sugar
1½ C. evaporated milk
⅔ C. chocolate chips
½ C. butter or oleo
1 tsp. vanilla

1 pkg. Oreo cookies
½ C. oleo (melted)
½ gallon vanilla ice cream
1½ C. salted Spanish peanuts

Boil first 5 ingredients for 8 minutes, stirring constantly; cool. Crush cookies and mix with ½ C. melted oleo. Spread in 9x13-inch pan. Spread ½ gallon softened ice cream over crust. Freeze till nearly solid and sprinkle peanuts over ice cream. Add chocolate mixture on top and freeze.

PISTACHIO ICE CREAM DESSERT

18 single graham crackers
   (2½x2½)

12 soda crackers
1 stick margarine

Crush crackers and mix margarine. Put in bottom of 9x13-inch pan.

BEAT AND MIX:
2 pkgs. instant pistachio pudding
2 C. milk

1 qt. softened vanilla ice cream

Pour mixture over cracker crust. Top with 1 pkg. Dream Whip and crush 2 Heath candy bars and sprinkle on top; refrigerate.

COCONUT CREAM DESSERT

1 C. margarine (melted)
2 C. flour
⅔ C. nuts (chopped)
3 C. cold milk
1 (8 oz.) pkg. cream cheese

1 C. powdered sugar
1 (9 oz.) carton whipped topping
2 pkgs. (30 oz.) instant coconut cream pudding mix

Mix margarine, flour, and nuts. Put in a 9x13-inch pan and bake at 350° for 15 to 20 minutes. Blend cream cheese and powdered sugar. Add 1 C. whipped topping. Spread over cooled crust. Combine both packages of pudding mix with milk. Spread over cheese mixture. Top with remaining whipped topping. Sprinkle with coconut and refrigerate until ready to use.

CHERRY DESSERT

2 cans cherry pie filling
Butter

2 boxes Jiffy cake mix

Put filling in an ungreased 9x13-inch pan. Pour dry cake mixes over fruit. Place pats of butter on top of cake mix. You can use any kind of filling and also add nuts to this. Bake at 350° for about 25 to 30 minutes, till top is brown.

PINK DESSERT

Crush 60 Ritz crackers and mix with ½ C. melted butter and ¼ C. powdered sugar. Put in 7½x11½-inch pan. Bake at 350° for 10 minutes.

For Filling: Mix 1 (10 oz.) carton Cool Whip, 1 can Eagle Brand sweetened condensed milk, and 1 (6 oz.) can pink lemonade. Pour over crust and refrigerate.

BUTTER PECAN DESSERT

1 C. graham cracker crumbs   1 stick melted oleo
1 C. soda cracker crumbs

Mix and press into 9x13-inch dish. Set aside (do not bake).

2 pkgs. instant vanilla pudding   1 qt. softened butter pecan
2 C. milk   or butter brickle ice cream

Beat pudding and milk. Add ice cream to pudding mixture. Put on top of prepared crust. Put Dream Whip prepared over top of pudding mixture. Cover with 1 (20 cent) heath candy bar that has been crushed. (Serves 12 to 15.)

CHOCOLATE AND VANILLA DESSERT

2 sq. chocolate   ½ C. butter
2 C. powdered sugar   3 eggs
1 tsp. vanilla   ½ C. nuts

Cream butter and powdered sugar; add melted chocolate and 3 egg yolks and vanilla. Beat egg whites stiff and fold in and add nuts. Line 9x13-inch pan with graham cracker crumbs and add above mixture and spread with vanilla ice cream as thick as desired and cover with graham cracker crumbs and freeze.

BANANA SPLIT DESSERT

2 C. crushed grahams
Butter
2 C. powdered sugar
1 tsp. vanilla
¼ C. crushed nuts

2 eggs (lightly beaten)
1 large can crushed pineapple
2 C. Cool Whip
Maraschino cherries

Combine cracker crumbs and 6 T. melted butter. Mix well and press into 9x13-inch pan. Combine ½ C. butter, sugar, vanilla, eggs, and beat till fluffy. Spread sugar mixture over crumb layer. Slice bananas lengthwise and arrange over sugar mixture. Spoon pineapple over bananas and cover pineapple layer with Cool Whip. Sprinkle with nuts and garnish with cherries. Chill for 6 hours before serving.

SODA CRACKER DESSERT

6 egg whites   ½ tsp. cream of tartar

Beat above until stiff. Beat in (small amount at a time) 2 C. of sugar. Fold in 2 C. broken soda crackers (not too fine). Add ¾ C. nutmeats. Grease a 9x13-inch pan. Bake at 350° for 25 minutes. Cool partially and cover with 2 C. of your favorite pie filling (cherry, black raspberry, etc.). Top with 2 C. whipped topping. Chill at least 6 hours before serving.

FROZEN DESSERT

1¼ C. graham cracker crumbs
2 T. sugar

¼ C. melted butter
A few grains of salt

Press this in the bottom of a 9x13-inch pan. Reserve a little for the topping. Now mix 2 boxes of instant vanilla pudding and 1⅓ C. milk. Chocolate or coconut cream puddings may also be used. Beat 3 C. softened vanilla ice cream into pudding for 4 minutes. Fold In 1 pkg. prepared Dream Whip. Place this on graham cracker crust and sprinkle top with crumbs and freeze.

MEATS

SALMON LOAF WITH CHEESY LEMON SAUCE

1 C. cracker crumbs
1 T. margarine (melted)
2 eggs
2 T. celery flakes
2 T. chopped onion
½ C. milk

1 can cream of chicken soup
1 (15½ oz.) can pink salmon
   (drained & flaked)
½ C. (2 oz.) shredded Casino
   Brand Natural Monterey Jack
   cheese

Combine all ingredients; mix well and pour into a greased casserole and smooth the surface. Bake at 350° for 45 minutes. Serve with Cheesy Lemon Sauce.

CHEESY LEMON SAUCE:
1 T. margarine
1 T. flour
½ C. milk
Salt & pepper

½ C. shredded Casino Brand
   Natural Monterey Jack cheese
½ tsp. lemon juice

Make a white sauce with margarine, flour, milk, and seasonings. Add cheese and stir until melted. Remove from heat and stir in lemon juice. Serve over top of salmon loaf.

SALMON PATTIES
(Makes approximately 22 patties.)

Make a thick white sauce as follows: Melt 4 T. butter or shortening. Add 4 T. flour. Stir until smooth. Stir in 1 C. milk and 1 tsp. salt. Cook until thick. Beat into white sauce 2 whole eggs, 1 (15 oz.) can salmon (Mackerel or tuna work fine also), 1 tsp. finely chopped onion or onion juice, and 1 ¼ C. cracker crumbs. Mix well and pack into a loaf pan and chill. (I prefer to make into patties on wax paper and chill). Roll in flour, then egg, then cracker crumbs and fry.

BEEF ROAST

Place 7-quart roaster on a medium to medium high burner. Place a piece of paper in pan. When the paper begins to burn, the pan is ready. Place the roast in the pan and brown for 4 minutes, turn the roast over and repeat browning for 4 minutes. Place vegetables on roast, place lid on top and turn to low heat. Any vegetables can be used but our family prefers carrots, onions, potatoes or cabbage. Cook over low heat for 90 minutes regardless of size of roast. This recipe is adaptable for pork which you cook twice as long or a frozen roast which you cook for 30 minutes longer. Besides the roast, Jack also cooks chicken without grease or flour. He doesn't broil or boil the chicken, yet it has a crispy crust.

SWEDISH SPARERIBS

1 T. salt	2 beef bouillon cubes
1 T. allspice	1 C. warm water
1 T. sugar	8-10 meaty spareribs
¼ C. oleo (oil or butter)	

Mix salt, allspice, and sugar; put in large plastic bag. Add spareribs and shake well so all meat is covered with mixture. Brown in large skillet until brown. Place in baking dish. Dissolve bouillon cubes in warm water. Pour over ribs. Cover and bake at 350° for an hour and 30 minutes.

BAR-B-CUED SPARE RIBS

Cut 3 lbs. spare ribs in serving pieces and put a little chopped onion and lemon on them. Nancy likes to put the ribs on to cook about noon or a little after, so that they cook for 4 to 5 hours. She sets the oven at 275° to 300° and cooks them with the lid on. About a half hour before you eat, take the lid off and turn the oven up to 350°. This browns the ribs and thickens the sauce. Before baking make the following sauce and pour over ribs:

2 T. brown sugar
1 tsp. paprika
1 tsp. salt
1 tsp. dry mustard
2 T. Worcestershire sauce
¼ tsp. chili powder

1/8 tsp. K-9 pepper (Nancy
    just uses reg. pepper here)
¼ C. vinegar
1 pt. stewed tomatoes
¼ C. catsup
½ C. water

BARBECUED SPARE RIBS

3 large bottles ketchup
1 box dark brown sugar
1 bottle Worcestershire sauce
2 cans tomato soup

5 tsp. chili powder
2 sliced onions
Season with salt

Place in 350° oven for 2½ hours or more. This recipe makes enough to barbecue 12 pounds of country style ribs.

SWEDISH SPARERIBS

1 T. salt
1 T. allspice
1 T. sugar
¼ C. oleo (oil or butter)

2 beef bouillon cubes
1 C. warm water
8-10 meaty spareribs

Mix salt, allspice, and sugar; put in large plastic bag. Add spareribs and shake well so all meat is covered with mixture. Brown in large skillet until brown. Place in baking dish. Dissolve bouillon cubes in warm water. Pour over ribs. Cover and bake at 350° for an hour and 30 minutes.

BAR-B-QUE BOLOGNA

1 can baked beans (pork & beans)
2 medium onions
½ lb. cheese (your favorite)

1 sq. cut from widest sheet
   of aluminum foil
1 large ring of bologna

Place ring of bologna in center of the foil, making sure the ends of bologna are tied together. Empty beans in middle of bologna. Make slits all the way around the ring of bologna. In each slit, place a wedge of cheese. Slice onions in thin slices and put on top of beans. Bring corners of foil together and twist. Place on grill and cook until onions are done and cheese is melted. To serve, place jacket in bowl and open. Easy and quick for summer meals.

SWEDISH MEATBALLS

1½ lbs. hamburger	1 tsp. salt
½ lb. seasoned sausage	Dash of pepper
1 egg	Onion
½ C. milk	1 can cream of mushroom soup
1 C. bread crumbs	

Beat egg and add milk and bread crumbs. Let stand a few minutes; add meat and seasoning. Add finely chopped onion. Form into small balls and brown in skillet. Cover with the can of soup and simmer for ½ hour.

PINEAPPLE BAKED BEEF BALLS

1 slice bread	2 T. chopped onion
½ C. water	1 can pineapple chunks
1 lb. beef	¼ C. green pepper (chopped)
1 tsp. salt	¼ C. catsup
1/8 tsp. pepper	2 T. vinegar

Soak bread in water. Combine beef, salt, pepper, and onion. Mix lightly and shape into 8 (1-inch) balls. Place ½-inch apart in a shallow baking dish. Bake at 375° for 20 minutes. Add drained pineapple chunks and green pepper. Blend catsup, vinegar, and 2 T. syrup drained from pineapple. Mix lightly with meatballs and pineapple. Continue baking for about 15 minutes longer until glazed. Makes 4 servings. May add 1 can of sweet potatoes when adding pineapple to make a complete meal.

PORK CHOPS SUPREME

Place chops in shallow Pan with ¼ C. water. Top with a slice of thin onion, 1 tsp. lemon juice, sprinkle with brown sugar and top with 1 T. catsup. Cover and bake at 350° for 45 to 50 minutes.

HOW TO BROIL LAMB CHOPS

Choose loin, rib or shoulder lamb chops, allowing 2 per person. Remove ''fell'' (the paperlike covering) if it is on chops. Diagonally slash outer edge of fat on meat at 1-inch intervals to prevent curling. Set oven control at broil and/ or 550°. Place chops in broiler pan; place broiler pan so tops of ¾ to 1-inch chops are 2-3 inches from heat, 1 to 2 inch chops are 3 to 5 inches from heat. Broil until brown. The chops should be about half done by this time. If desired, season chops with salt and pepper. (Always season after browning as salt draws moisture to surface and delays browning.) Turn chops and broil until brown. Timetable for broiling lamb chops: 1-inch for 12 minutes; 1½ inches for 18 minutes or 2 inches for 22 minutes.

GROUND HAM MEAT BALLS

1 lb. hamburger	3 C. graham cracker crumbs
1 lb. sausage	3 eggs
2¼ lb. ground ham	2 C. milk

Combine ingredients and make balls.

2 cans tomato soup	2 tsp. mustard
½ C. vinegar	2½ C. brown sugar
¼ C. water	

Combine and pour over balls. Bake at 350° for 1½ hours. Serves 12 to 15.

CHILI CHICKEN

1 cut-up chicken	1 C. milk
2 C. flour	Dash of Tabasco sauce
2 T. chili powder	2 T. Worcestershire sauce

Mix chicken, flour, and chili powder together. Then mix milk, Tabasco sauce, and 2 T. Worcestershire sauce. Line a 9x12-inchd pan with foil and put a stick of oleo in it. Place in oven until it melts - at 350°. Dip chicken in liquid mix, then in flour mix. Put in 350° for ½ hour on one side, turn and bake another ½ hour.

SWEDISH MEAT BALLS

1 C. milk
½ C. bread crumbs
½ lb. ground round
½ lb. ground sausage
1 egg
1 tsp. salt
¼ tsp. pepper

1 T. steak sauce
1 T. instant minced onion
2 T. shortening
¼ C. flour
1 C. water
2 tsp. instant bouillon

Pour milk over bread crumbs and let sit for 15 minutes. Mix in meat, egg, and seasoning. Make 12 balls. Preheat browning skillet for 4½ minutes. Melt shortening in skillet. Brown and turn. Remove from pan and sprinkle flour into shortening. Stir until smooth. Blend in water and bouillon, stirring constantly. Heat in microwave for 3 minutes, stirring every 30 seconds. Place balls in gravy, cover and cook for 3 additional minutes.

HAMBURGER FOR GRILL

(If you like a little zip in your grilled hamburgers try this.)

1 lb. hamburger
¾ tsp. instant onion
Salt & pepper, to taste

¼ tsp. garlic salt
¼ tsp. oregano

Form into hamburger patties and grill. Garlic salt and oregano are also good on steak from the grill.

PATIO CHICKEN BARBECUE

1 (8 oz.) can (1 C.) tomato sauce
½ C. water
¼ C. molasses
2 T. butter
2 T. vinegar
2 T. minced onion

1 T. Worcestershire sauce
2 tsp. dry mustard
1 tsp. salt
¼ tsp. pepper
¼ tsp. chili powder

Brush in salad oil, salt, and pepper. In saucepan, combine tomato sauce, water, molasses, butter, vinegar, onion, and Worcestershire sauce, dry mustard, salt, pepper, and chili powder. Simmer and mix for 15 to 20 minutes; set aside. Brush chicken with salad oil and season with salt and pepper. Place bone side down on grill. Broil over slow coals for 25 minutes, turnning occasionally and basting, turning occasionally for 10 to 15 minutes till tender.

PORK CHOPS WITH PAPRIKA-DILL SAUCE

6 shoulder pork chops
  (about ¾-inch thick)
½ C. flour, seasoned with salt &
  pepper, to taste
4 T. butter or margarine
4 medium onions
  (chopped or sliced)

2 cloves of garlic (minced)
2 T. paprika, to taste
1 chicken bouillon cube,
  dissolved in 1 C. boiling water
1 C. sour cream
2 tsp. dried dillweed

Dredge chops in seasoned flour (reserve 2 T.). Heat butter in large skillet and brown chops on both sides; set aside. Add onions and garlic to skillet and saute over medium heat for 6 to 8 minutes or until tender, stirring occasionally. Stir in paprika and bouillon and cook over high heat to deglaze skillet. Add chops and bring to boil; reduce heat, cover, and simmer for 45 minutes or until chops are tender. Remove chops to heated serving dish and keep warm. Blend sour cream and 2 T. reserved flour; stir in dillweed. Then stir into onion mixture and cook. Stir over medium heat just until sauce thickens and is smooth (do not boil). Ladle some sauce over chops and serve remainder in sauce dish. Good with noodles and rolls. Serves 6.

PORK CHOPS POTATO BAKE

5 or 6 pork chops
Raw, sliced potatoes
Salt & pepper

Minced onion
1 can cream of mushroom soup
1 can Cheddar cheese soup

Brown pork chops. Slice enough potatoes to half fill a 9x13-inch buttered pan. Sprinkle with salt, pepper, and onion, to taste. Combine soups and pour half over potatoes. Lay pork chops over potatoes and cover with remaining soup. Bake, covered at 350° for 1 hour or until potatoes are done. Uncover and bake until brown.

GLORIFIED GROUND BEEF

1 lb. ground beef
½ C. dry bread crumbs
1 beaten egg
1 tsp. salt
1/8 tsp. pepper

2 T. minced onion
½ C. finely chopped celery
1 can cream of mushroom or
   chicken soup
½ C. water

Combine first 7 ingredients and shape in oval patty about an inch thick. Using small amount of butter brown on both sides in skillet. Combine soup and water; pour over and around meat. Cook slowly in covered skillet for about 25 minutes. Small potatoes or potato slices around the meat is delicious. Soup and meat juices will make the gravy.

GRAVY BAKED PORK CHOPS

¼ tsp. salt
Dash of pepper
4-6 lean pork chops
1 T. shortening

1 can cream of chicken soup
⅔ C. canned milk
⅓-½ C. water
1 onion (chopped)

Sprinkle salt and pepper over chops. Melt shortening in pan. Brown chops on both sides; drain off fat. Mix soup, milk, water, and onion. Pour over chops and bake at 350° for 45 minutes or until chops are tender. Stir gravy well. Serve with mashed potatoes.

CHICKEN CONFETTI

4-5 lbs. broiler-fryer chicken
  (cut-up)
1 tsp. salt
1/8 tsp. pepper
¼ C. salad oil
½ C. chopped onion
1 clove garlic
2 cans (16 oz. ea.) tomatoes
1 (8 oz.) can tomato sauce

1 (6 oz.) can tomato paste
2 T. snipped parsley
2 tsp. salt
1 tsp. basil
¼ tsp. pepper
7 or 8 oz. spaghetti
  (cooked & drained)
Grated Parmesan cheese

Wash chicken pieces and pat dry. Season with 1 tsp. salt and 1/8 tsp. pepper. In large skillet or Dutch oven, brown chicken in oil; remove chicken. Pour off all but 3 T. fat. Add onion and garlic. Cook and stir till onion is tender. Stir in chicken and remaining ingredients except spaghetti and cheese. Cover tightly; cook chicken slowly for 1 to 1½ hours or till tender, stir occasionally and add water, if necessary. Skim off excess fat. Serve on spaghetti and sprinkle with Parmesan cheese. Makes 4 to 6 servings.

SKILLET PORK CHOPS 'N' RICE

1 medium onion (sliced)
¼ C. sliced celery
2 T. vegetable oil
4 pork chops (½-inch thick)
1 C. uncooked rice
Salt & pepper, to taste

1½ C. water
2 T. brown sugar
½ tsp. salt
¼ tsp. pepper
2 cans (8 oz. ea.) tomato sauce

Saute onions and celery lightly in oil. Sprinkle chops with salt and pepper. Add to skillet and brown on both sides. Remove chops. Add water, brown sugar, salt, pepper, and 1½ cans tomato sauce to skillet. Heat and stir, bring to boiling point. Add rice to skillet and stir. (There will be a lot of liquid, but the rice will absorb it.) Put chops into this mixture, cover skillet and simmer for 30 minutes. Pour remaining sauce over chops. Cover and cook for 15 minutes longer. Makes 4 servings.

BARBECUED SPARE RIBS

4 lbs. spare ribs
4 T. onions (minced)
1 C. tomato sauce
¾ C. water
3 T. vinegar
2 T. Worcestershire sauce

1 tsp. salt
1 tsp. pepper
¼ tsp. cinnamon
Dash of cloves
½ C. brown sugar

Brown ribs. Heat remaining ingredients to a boil, pour over ribs and bake covered at 325° for 1½ hours.

CHICKEN DIVAN

1 chicken (cooked & picked
  from the bone)
1 large bag of frozen broccoli
  (cooked)

1 can Cheddar cheese soup
  that's been thinned with
  ¾ C. milk

Mix all together and bake for ½ hour or until hot clear through.

CHICKEN NOUGATS

4 whole chicken breasts
½ C. fine dry bread crumbs
   (unseasoned)
¼ C. grated Parmesan cheese

2 tsp. Accent
1 tsp. salt
1 tsp. thyme
½ C. melted margarine

Cook and bone chicken, remove skin. Cut into small pieces. Combine bread, cheese, Accent, salt, and herbs. Dip chicken into margarine, then in crumbs. Place in foil-lined baking sheet. Bake at 400° for 15 minutes.

SWEET AND SOUR PORK

1 ½ lbs. pork shoulder
   (cut in 2'' strips)
½ tsp. salt
1 T. cooking oil
¾ C. water
1 lge. can pineapple chunks
3 T. brown sugar
Rice

¼ tsp. ginger
3 T. cornstarch
¼ C. vinegar
2 T. soy sauce
1 medium green pepper
   (cut in 2'' strips)
1 medium onion (sliced)

Brown salted pork in oil, add water and bring to boil. Cover and simmer 1 hour. Drain pineapple (save juice). Add enough water to juice to make 1 ¼ C. Combine juice, brown sugar, ginger, cornstarch, vinegar and soy sauce; gradually stir into meat. Cook until slightly thickened. Add green pepper, onion and pineapple. Cover, simmer 5 minutes. Serve over rice.

HEAD CHEESE

1 hog's head	Sage and chili powder
1 hog's tongue	Salt and pepper

Clean and scrape hog's head; wash thoroughly. Wash and trim hog's tongue. Cover head and tongue with slightly salted water. Simmer until meat falls from bone. Drain meat; shred. Season to taste; mix thoroughly. Pack tightly in bowl. Cover and weigh down. Let stand 3 days.

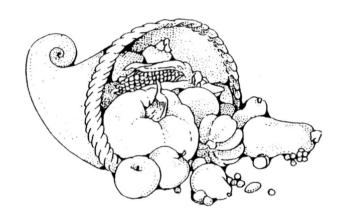

CHICKEN WINGS

24 chicken wings	⅓ C. brown sugar
10-oz. soy sauce	1 tsp. ground nutmeg
1 tsp. ginger	Garlic powder

Marinate chicken wings in the following overnight: soy sauce, ginger, brown sugar, and ground mustard. Bake 1½ hours at 350°, turning every 15 minutes. When done sprinkle with garlic powder and return to oven for a few minutes.

MOCK CHICKEN LEGS

1 lb. round steak
1 lb. pork steak

2 eggs (beaten well)
2 C. soda cracker crumbs
(crushed)

Cut steak into 1 ½-2-inch cubes and place alternately 6 cubes on a wooden skewer. Roll in egg and then in cracker crumbs. Brown in a skillet with a little shortening. Place in roaster with lid and bake at 350° for 1 ½ hours. Uncover and bake 30 more minutes or until crisp and brown. The juice in the bottom of the roaster makes excellent gravy.

WILD STIR-FRY CHICKEN SKILLET

2 T. vegetable oil
2 C. water
1 (6 ¼ oz.) pkg. Uncle Ben's fast
cooking long grain rice
½ C. chopped onion

4 chicken breasts (skinned, boned
and cut into bite-size pieces)
½ tsp. salt
1 medium tomato (chopped)
2 C. shredded lettuce

Heat oil; add chicken and cook, stirring frequently, until firm and white. Add water, rice and seasoning packets, onion, salt. Bring to a boil. Reduce heat, cover and simmer until water is absorbed, about 15 minutes. Stir in lettuce and tomato just before serving. (I substitute canned chicken.)

CASHEW CHICKEN

2 whole chicken breasts
  (skinned and boned; 4 pieces)
1 clove garlic (minced or pressed)
½ tsp. curry powder
4 T. butter or margarine
⅓ C. salted cashews

¼ C. apple juice or dry sherry
1½ T. cornstarch
1 tsp. salt
1 lb. mushrooms (sliced)
1 C. whipping cream
¼ C. parsley

Slice chicken strips ½-inch wide. Place in bowl. Add apple juice or sherry, corn-starch, garlic, salt and curry, tossing well. Set aside to marinate for 15 minutes. Saute mushrooms in 2 T. of butter for 2 minutes or until brown. Remove from pan. Add remaining butter to pan over high heat. Add chicken slices. Saute quickly for 5-10 minutes or until pieces are golden. Add mushrooms to chicken. Toss over high heat for 30 seconds. Add cream. Cook, stirring until cream is boiled down and thickened. Transfer to serving dish. Sprinkle with cashews and parsley. Serve over hot cooked rice.

CHICKEN CASSEROLE

1 boiled chicken with broth

1 stalk celery
⅓ C. butter

1 onion

Saute until tender.

6 C. bread crumbs
2 eggs
1½ C. milk

Sage to taste
½ tsp. baking powder

Mix together. Add broth to proper consistency. Bake in 350° oven for about 1 hour or until browned. Cream of chicken soup (do not thin with water) served as a topping is delicious.

PIES &
PASTRIES

BANANA MALLOW PIE

CRUST:
2 C. shredded coconut   ⅓ C. oleo (melted)

FILLING:
1 (3¼ oz.) instant vanilla pudding   2 or 3 bananas (sliced)
2 C. Cool Whip   1½ C. miniature marshmallows
1¾ C. milk

Combine coconut and margarine in skillet. Cook over low heat, stirring frequently till coconut is toasted and golden brown. Press into 9-inch pie pan and chill. Prepare pudding using 1¾ C. milk. Fold in Cool Whip and marshmallows. Slice bananas into cooled crust. Pour pudding mixture over bananas. Chill for several hours. Garnish with banana slices and whole pecans. This recipe is very easy.

CHERRY ANGEL PIE

3 egg whites (room temp.)   1 (3½ oz.) pkg. vanilla instant
1/8 tsp. cream of tartar   pudding
1/8 tsp. salt   1¼ C. milk
¾ C. sugar   ¾ tsp. almond flavoring
¼ tsp. vanilla   1 can cherry pie filling

In small bowl with mixer at high speed, beat egg whites, cream of tartar and salt until soft peaks form; gradually sprinkle in sugar 2 T. at a time, beating until each addition is completely dissolved. (Whites should stand in stiff, glossy peaks.) Beat in vanilla. Spoon meringue into a well-greased 9-inch pie plate, smoothing it in the center and high on the sides to form a pie shell. (Or you can form the pie shell without a dish and bake it on a jelly-roll pan covered with brown paper for easier serving.) Bake shell for 1 hour and 15 minutes; cool. Prepare instant pudding as label directs but use only 1¼ C. milk. Stir in almond flavoring and pour into meringue crust. Spoon pie filling over pudding; chill. May garnish with whipped cream.

POPOVERS

1 C. sifted flour
½ tsp. salt

1 C. milk
2 eggs

Beat the above ingredients with a rotary beater just until smooth. Pour into well-greased heated muffin tins. Thelma places ⅓ tsp. butter in each cup before heating the tin. Bake at 425° for 30 to 35 minutes. This recipe makes 8 or 9 so Thelma usually uses 1½ times the recipe for 1 dozen rolls.

DUTCH LETTERS

CHILL OVERNIGHT:
1 lb. oleo
4 C. flour

1 tsp. salt
1 C. cold water

Also chill overnight.

FILLING:
2 C. almond paste
2 C. sugar
2 tsp. almond flavor

4 eggs
¾ C. bread crumbs

Roll crust into 12 strips. Put filling on dough and roll up. Brush with egg white and sprinkle with sugar. Bake at 400° for about 20 minutes.

Peach Pie

¾ C. sugar (can use ¼ C. brown
   sugar for part of the ¾ C.)
2 to 3 T. flour
¼ tsp. cinnamon

5 C. peeled, sliced, fresh peaches
   or use canned peaches
2 T. butter or margarine
1 pastry shell
Pastry for lattice top

Combine sugar, flour, and cinnamon; add to peaches and mix lightly. Spread into a 9-inch pastry shell. Dot with butter before or after adjusting lattice top. Flute the edges. If you prefer a full top crust, you can sprinkle top with sugar. Bake in hot oven (400°) for 45 to 50 minutes. Cool before cutting.

Custard Pumpkin Pie

1 C. pumpkin
3 eggs (separated)
1 tsp. ginger
½ tsp. cinnamon

½ tsp. nutmeg
1 C. milk
½ C. sugar
Pinch of salt

Beat egg whites stiff and fold into pumpkin mixture. Pour into unbaked pie shell. Bake at 425° for 15 minutes and at 350° for 35 minutes. Serve with whipped cream.

CHERRY PUFF

1 (1 lb. 5 oz.) can cherry pie
  filling
1 tsp. almond extract
2 eggs (separated)
¼ tsp. cream of tartar

⅓ C. white sugar
Dash of salt
¼ C. plus 2 T. sifted cake
  flour

In small bowl mix pie filling and extract. Then pour into buttered 1½-quart casserole. In small bowl beat egg whites and cream of tartar at high speed till foamy. Gradually add sugar. Beat till stiff. In large bowl, with fork beat egg yolks with salt. Add whites into yolks and fold, then fold in cake flour. Pour mixture over filling and bake for 1 hour.

Superior Pumpkin Pie Filling

1½ C cooked pumpkin
⅔ C. firmly packed brown sugar
2 eggs
½ tsp. ginger

1 tsp. cinnamon
½ tsp. salt
1½ C. milk or
  evaporated milk

Mix together well. Pour into pie shell and bake at 425° for 15 minutes and at 325° for 45 minutes or until knife comes out clean.

DATE AND NUT PINWHEELS

COOK THE FOLLOWING:
1⅓ C. dates (chopped)   ½ C. water
½ C. sugar   ½ C. nuts

THEN CREAM:
⅔ C. shortening   2 eggs (beaten)
1⅓ C. brown sugar

SIFT:
½ tsp. salt   2⅔ C. flour
½ tsp. soda

Roll out ¼-inch thick into two rectangles. Spread with dates. Roll up and chill overnight. Then slice and bake at 375° until lightly brown.

ELEPHANT EARS

½ C. milk (scalded)   2 T. sugar
¼ C. warm water   ½ tsp. salt
1 pkg. yeast   ½ C. softened butter
2 C. flour   1 egg yolk

TOPPING:
1½ C. sugar   1 T. cinnamon

Combine flour, 2 T. sugar, and salt. Cut in ½ C. butter as for pastry. Add egg yolk and scalded and cooled milk. Soften the yeast in the warm water and add to mixture. Chill 2 or more hours with a half hour in the freezer. Roll to 10x18-inches. Brush with melted butter and sprinkle with cinnamon and sugar. Roll as for cinnamon rolls and cut into 18 pieces. Put cinnamon and sugar mixture on waxed paper and roll one piece at a time. Put roll between waxed paper and flatten with a rolling pin. Brush with melted butter again and sprinkle with nuts and more sugar and cinnamon. Bake on a well-greased cookie sheet for 12 minutes at 400°. Cool on waxed paper or rack. I usually make a double batch as they go so fast.

SALADS

7 LAYER JELLO SALAD

Use 3 oz. pkg. Jello for each layer.

Black cherry - water layer	Orange - water layer
Cherry - milk layer	Orange-pineapple - milk layer
Lime - water layer	Strawberry - water layer
Lemon - milk layer	

Mix Jello with water or milk (as indicated).

WATER LAYER:
¾ C. hot water   ¾ C. cold water

MILK LAYER:
½ C. hot water   ½ C. evaporated milk
½ C. cold water

After last layer is set, prepare Dream Whip or Cool Whip and spread on top. These set up rather fast, especially the milk layers, so will have to be watched closely. Should be poured on each firm layer when partially congealed. (Glenda uses raspberry Jello instead of strawberry.)

131

PISTACHIO PUDDING SALAD

1 pkg. instant pistachio
   pudding mix
1½ C. milk
1 tall can crushed pineapple

2 C. colored marshmallows
9 oz. container Cool Whip
1 C. maraschino cherries
   (cut-up)

Combine milk and pudding mix, then add rest of ingredients. Save some cherries to put on top.

RIBBON SALAD

1 (3 oz.) pkg. lemon Jello
1 (3 oz.) pkg. lime Jello
1 (3 oz.) pkg. raspberry Jello
3 C. boiling water
1 C. miniature marshmallows
1½ C. cold water

2 pkgs. (3 oz. ea.) softened
   cream cheese
½ C. mayonnaise
1 C. whipped cream
1 small can crushed pineapple
   (drained)

Dissolve Jello flavors separately, using 1 C. boiling water for each. Stir marshmallows into lemon Jello; set aside. Add ¾ C. cold water to lime Jello and pour into 9x13-inch pan. Chill till set but not firm. Add ¾ C. cold water to raspberry Jello; set aside at room temperature. Then add cream cheese to lemon Jello mixture; beat until blended. Chill till slightly thickened. Then blend in mayonnaise, whipped cream, and pineapple. Chill until very thick, spoon gently over lime Jello. Chill till set, but not firm. Meanwhile chill raspberry Jello till thickened and pour over lemon mixture. Chill till firm.

PRETZEL SALAD

1ST LAYER:

2½ C. pretzels   ¾ C. butter (melted)

3 T. powdered sugar

Mix together and press in bottom of 9x13-inch pan. Bake at 350° for 10 minutes; cool.

2ND LAYER:

1 large sq. (8 oz.) cream cheese   1 C. powdered sugar

1 egg

Beat together, then fold in 1 (9 oz.) container of Cool Whip. Spread on cooled first layer. Put in refrigerator to cool.

3RD LAYER:

2 C. boiling water   2 boxes (small) strawberry Jello

Mix, then add 2 boxes of frozen strawberries, thicken, then spread on top of 2nd layer. Put in the refrigerator.

QUICK AND EASY SALAD

2 C. cottage cheese   1 small can mandarin oranges

1 pkg. dry Jello (any flavor)   (drained)

1 small can crushed pineapple   1 small container Cool Whip

    (drained)

Mix together and refrigerate.

SURPRISE MACARONI SALAD

1 env. plain gelatin
1 C. milk
1 C. mayonnaise
1 carton cottage cheese
1 T. prepared mustard
1 C. uncooked macaroni
1 C. diced ham

1 C. diced sharp Cheddar
  cheese
½ C. diced green pepper
½ C. sliced celery
½ C. sliced green onion
¼ C. chopped pimento
Large leaf lettuce or spinach
  leaves

Cook macaroni and set aside. Soften gelatin in milk in large saucepan, cook over moderate heat, stirring constantly until gelatin dissolves; cool. Pour ¼ C. gelatin mixture into 6 cup mold; add some ham, cheese, and green pepper to make top design. Chill until firm. Stir mayonnaise, cottage cheese, and mustard into remaining gelatin mixture. Fold in macaroni, ham, Cheddar cheese, green pepper, celery, green onion, and pimento. Spoon mixture into mold on top of set layer; refrigerate until firm. To unmold, loosen gelatin from side of mold with long sharp knife. Quickly immerse in bowl of hot water. Invert onto lettuce or spinach leaves.

MARINATED CARROT SALAD

1 (2 lb.) bag carrots
  (cooked & cool)
1 green pepper
  (chopped or diced fine)
1 onion (chopped fine)
Several stalks of celery (diced or sliced)

1 can tomato soup
1 tsp. prepared mustard
½ C. oil
¾ C. vinegar
1 tsp. salt & 1 C. sugar

Mix tomato soup, prepared mustard, oil, sugar, salt, and vinegar; bring to a boil. Pour over vegetables. Marinate in refrigerator for at least 24 hours. Keep in refrigerator for a week or more. Drain off juice to serve.

SPIRIT OF '76 SALAD

BOTTOM LAYER:
Mix 1 large box strawberry Jello, dissolved with 2 C. boiling water. Add 1 box frozen strawberries; let set.

2ND LAYER:
1 pkg. Dream Whip (whipped up)   1 C. miniature marshmallows
1 C. sour cream

TOP LAYER:
1 can blueberry pie filling or fresh blueberries.

FROSTED SALAD

2 pkgs. Lemon gelatin   1 (No 2) can crushed pineapple
2 C. boiling water   2 bananas
2 C. 7-Up   ½ lb. marshmallows

Dissolve gelatin in boiling water; add 7-Up and chill. Mix fruit and marshmallows. Add to gelatin; chill till firm.

TOPPING:
½ C. sugar   1 egg (beaten)
2 T. flour   1 C. Dream Whip
2 T. butter   ½ C. grated cheese
1 C. pineapple juice

Combine flour, sugar, butter, egg, and juice. Cook until thick; cool and fold in Dream Whip. Spread on salad and sprinkle with cheese; chill.

SUMMER SALAD

2 C. creamed cottage cheese
¼ tsp. dry mustard
2 tsp. caraway seed

½ tsp. salt
¼ tsp. pepper
1 T. Capers (optional)

Combine the above and then prepare the following:

1 medium green pepper (diced)
¼ C. diced green onions
1 C. diced celery

¼ C. diced radishes
¼ C. chopped pimentos
 (optional)

Combine and chill for 1 to 2 hours, then mound on a bed of lettuce. Surround with hard boiled eggs and quartered ripe tomatoes. Berdine uses 2 hard boiled eggs and 2 tomatoes. Serves 4. This is a milk salad that goes well with spicy barbecued foods or for a luncheon main dish.

SAUERKRAUT SALAD

Drain 1 large can kraut and run cold water over it to make it crisp.

ADD:
½ C. vinegar
1⅓ C. sugar
½ C. salad oil
1 C. diced celery
1 small onion (diced)

1 red pimiento (diced)
 (if you use sweet pickle)
½ C. pickles or about 1 dozen
 stuffed olives
 (sliced crossways)

Mix oil, vinegar, and sugar well. Add remaining ingredients and let stand in refrigerate overnight. This keeps indefinitely. Make sure it has a tight lid.

PINK SALAD

2 pkgs. strawberry or raspberry
    Jello

1 C. sugar
1 (9 oz.) container Cool Whip

Prepare Jello in large bowl as directed. Refrigerate until Jello is set. With mixer add sugar and Cool Whip. Mix until smooth. Refrigerate until set in bowl or 13x9-inch pan. (Shirley said this is a recipe lids love.)

SPRING BREEZE SALAD

2 (3 oz. ea.) pkgs. lime Jello
1 (3 oz.) pkg. lemon Jello
1 C. boiling water
3 C. cold liquid
    (fruit juices plus water)
1 can lemon pie filling

1 large can crushed pineapple
    (drained)
1 pkg. Dream Whip
1 large can fruit cocktail
    (drained)

Dissolve Jello in boiling water; add fruit juices. Immediately beat in pie filling. Reserve 1 C. mixture and place rest in refrigerator to chill. When Jello starts to congeal; add fruits and pour into a 9x13-inch pan; chill. Beat Dream Whip as directed. Blend reserve mixture into prepared Dream Whip and spread over salad.

CRISPY SPRING SALAD

VEGETABLES: (Chopped or Diced)
1 head cauliflower
Radishes
Small onions
Celery

Carrots
Green peppers
Or any crunchy vegetables

DRESSING:
1 C. sour cream
½ C. salad dressing

1 pkg. dry Italian Good Seasons
    dressing

Mix and put over vegetables.

LIME SALAD

2 pkgs. lime Jello, dissolved in
  2 C. hot water
4 C. vanilla ice cream

1 can or 2 C. crushed
  pineapple

Stir until ice cream is melted. Add nuts, if desired.

LIME JELLO SALAD

1 pkg. lime Jello
15 large marshmallows

1 C. boiling water

Stir all together and set in boiling water till marshmallows dissolve. Let cool.

1 C. whip cream
1 C. cottage cheese (small curds)

1 C. pineapple (crushed)
½ C. chopped nuts

When Jello has begun to congeal add the second mixture and mix well. Serve on lettuce.

SPINACH SALAD

2 pkgs. frozen chopped spinach
  (thaw and drain)
½ C. chopped celery

1 C. sharp Cheddar cheese
2 hard-boiled eggs (chopped)
½ C. chopped onions

Mix above together.

DRESSING:
2 tsp. horseradish
2 tsp. vinegar

½ tsp. salt
¾ C. salad dressing

Mix and put in above; mix well.

SOUPS & SANDWICHES

FRUIT-CHEESE TOAST

¼ C. butter
3 eggs
3 T. milk
8 slices whole wheat bread
3 oz. cream cheese (softened)

1 apple or pear or peach or
   banana
½ tsp. lemon juice
¼ C. raisins
Honey (optional)

Heat oven to 450°. Melt butter in a jelly roll pan in oven and spread evenly. Beat 2 whole eggs and 1 egg white with milk. Dip bread in egg mixture, coating both sides, then put bread in buttered pan. Bake for 5 minutes. Mix cream cheese and egg yolk. Chop fruit and add lemon juice and raisins. Remove bread from oven. Turn and spread each slice with cheese mixture. Top with fruit. Bake for 5 more minutes or until cheese is set and fruit is tender. Honey is good on top.

HOMEMADE BEAN SOUP

1 lb. dried beans
Water
1 meaty ham hock or pork bones
½ C. chopped onion
2 cloves garlic (minced)
1 C. chopped celery
½ C. chopped carrots

¼ C. chopped parsley
1½ tsp. salt
½ tsp. pepper
1 tsp. nutmeg
1 tsp. oregano
1 tsp. basil
1 bay leaf

Place beans in large kettle and add 6 to 8 C. hot water. Bring to boil and boil for 2 minutes. Remove from heat, cover and let stand for 1 hour. Drain and add 2 quarts of cold water and hock. Bring to boil and simmer for 1½ hours. Stir in remaining ingredients and simmer for 20 to 30 minutes until beans are tender. Remove hock and trim off meat and return to soup. Note: Do not add salt if cured pork is used.

VEGETABLE BEEF SOUP

2 T. cooking oil or oleo   1½-2 lbs. stew meat

Put cooking oil and stew meat in slow cooker and let cook for 2 hours approximately. It will form a lot of juice.

ADD:
2 C. diced potatoes   1 tsp. salt
½ C. chopped onion or   3 tsp. instant beef bouillon
   2 tsp. instant minced onion   1 tsp. celery salt
1 qt. tomato juice   ¼ C. rice
1 tsp. sugar

Let all slow cook for several hour. One half hour before serving, add 2 cans Veg-All (mixed vegetables). If it seems too thick to suit you, a little water can be added.

EGG SALAD SANDWICHES

6 hard-cooked eggs   ½ C. mayonnaise
   (finely chopped)   1 tsp. salt
½ C. finely cut-up celery   Bread
¼ C. pickle relish (well-drained)

Mix all ingredients, except bread in a medium bowl. Cover the mixture and refrigerate until ready to make the sandwiches. Make open sandwiches and top with a thin tomato slice or place between two slices of buttered bread. Makes about 2½ cups or enough for 8 sandwiches.

BARBECUED BEEF

3-4 lbs. roast (cooked & chopped)   ¾ C. brown sugar
1 C. chopped celery   ½ tsp. salt
½ C. onion (minced)   1 C. water or broth
1½ C. catsup

Simmer for 1½ hours. Good for hot sandwiches or just as a main course with potatoes.

VEGETABLE BEEF SOUP

In an electric skillet, brown 1 chuck roast and cook till done. (You can serve the roast to your family for one meal and use the remainder for the soup.) Fill a large kettle half full of water and add 1 T. of salt. Peel and slice in pieces:

6 large potatoes
1 onion
2 or 3 stalks of celery

4 large carrots
1 pkg. green beans

Let the vegetables cook in the water till half done, then add the chopped up roast and broth and one package of peas if you like. Also, a little celery seed and onion salt add more flavor, as do parsley flakes and pepper. Add more salt, to taste. Cover and simmer until nice and done, about ½ an hour or so.

MOM'S POTATO SOUP

Peel 6 to 7 good-sized potatoes. Chop 2 onions. Saute these in ¼-½ C. butter. Then add 3 to 4 C. milk; add celery seed, to taste. Add 2 tsp. sugar, salt, and pepper to taste. Cook over low heat for 1½ hours or until done.

MANWICHES

1½ lbs. browned hamburger
1 chopped onion
1 can tomato soup
1 T. vinegar
2 T. water

1 T. brown sugar
1 tsp. chili powder
1 T. Worcestershire sauce
¼ tsp. celery salt
Salt & pepper

Simmer for 20 minutes.

BARBECUE ROAST BEEF

1 C. catsup   ½ tsp. salt
2 T. brown sugar   ½ tsp. dry mustard
1 T. steak sauce   3 C. cooked roast beef (diced)

In saucepan stir together first 5 ingredients; add diced beef. Cover and simmer for 10 to 15 minutes. Serve on buns.

4 BEAN SOUP

1 lb. ground beef   1 can navy beans
½ lb. bacon   1 can great Northern beans
2 medium onions (chopped)   1 C. ketchup
1 C. brown sugar   ½ C. mustard
1 can kidney beans   4 T. Worcestershire sauce
1 can pork & beans   4 T. liquid smoke

(Do not drain beans.) Brown ground beef and onions, drain cooked bacon and crumble. Mix all together and put in crock pot on low or in oven at 375° for 1 hour.

CORNBEEF SANDWICH

1 can cornbeef   ½ env. dry onion soup mix
1 carton sour cream

Put on bun. Put a slice of Swiss cheese on top and wrap in tin foil. Heat in 400° oven for 10 to 15 minutes. Makes 24 mini-buns.

VEGETABLES

ONION PATTIES

¾ C. flour
1 T. cornmeal
1 T. sugar
1 tsp. salt

2 tsp. baking powder
¾ C. milk
2½ C. finely chopped onion

Mix the dry ingredients. Add milk, then onions. Batter will be thick. Drop by spoonfuls into hot grease. Turn once, so each side is golden brown.

CABBAGE CASSEROLE

1 small head of cabbage
1 lb. hamburger
1 small onion (chopped)

¼ C. uncooked rice
1 can tomato soup
1 can water

Cut cabbage in ½-inch wedges and put in casserole. Brown meat and onions; stir in rice and put over cabbage. Mix soup in water, heat and pour over all. Bake at 350° for 1½ hours.

COMPANY CARROTS

4 C. sliced peeled carrots
1 T. chopped onion
3 T. butter
1 can cream of celery soup
½ tsp. salt

1/8 tsp. pepper
½ C. grated Cheddar cheese
2½ C. herb-flavored croutons
⅓ C. melted butter or oleo

Cook carrots in boiling water and drain. Meanwhile, cook onion in 3 T. butter until soft. Stir in soup, salt, pepper, cheese, and carrots. Place in greased 2-quart casserole. Toss bread croutons with ⅓ C. melted butter. Spoon over carrots. Bake at 350° until thoroughly heated - about 20 minutes. Makes 6 servings.

BROCCOLI LIMA CASSEROLE

3 T. butter
2 T. Cheez Whiz
2½ C. Rice Chex
1 pkg. frozen broccoli

1 pkg. lima beans
1 can mushroom soup
1 can celery soup

Melt butter; add Rice Chex, brown slightly and set aside to cool. Cook vegetable as directed on package. Combine Cheese Whiz to soups and add lima beans. Stir and add 1 C. of the cereal mixture. Add broccoli and place in buttered dish. Top with remaining cereal. Bake at 350° for 30 minutes.

BROCCOLI AND RICE CASSEROLE

2 C. frozen broccoli
(cooked & drained)
2 C. loosely packed cooked
Minute Rice (season with
butter & lemon juice)

1 can mushroom soup
2 cubes chicken bouillon,
dissolved in ⅔ C. of water

Mix altogether lightly and add mushrooms, if desired. Bake at 300° for 20 minutes (cover lightly). Can be prepared a day ahead and refrigerated.

THREE BEAN CASSEROLE

1 can green beans
1 can kidney beans
1 can butter beans

1 can cream of mushroom soup
1 can onion rings

Drain beans well and toss together in 1½-quart casserole dish. Pour un-diluted soup over the beans. Cover and bake at 325° for 1½ hours. Remove and spread onion rings over top. Return to oven for 15 minutes.

To Order Copies

Please send me _____ copies of *Amish Ladies Cookbook for Amish Ladies with Old Husbands* at $9.95 each plus $3.50 S/H. (Make checks payable to Hearts 'N Tummies Cookbooks.)

Name _____

Street _____

City _____ State _____ Zip _____

Hearts 'N Tummies Cookbook Co.
3544 Blakslee St.
Wever IA   52658
1-800-571-2665

To Order Copies

Please send me _____ copies of *Amish Ladies Cookbook for Amish Ladies with Old Husbands* at $9.95 each plus $3.50 S/H. (Make checks payable to Hearts 'N Tummies Cookbooks.)

Name _____

Street _____

City _____ State _____ Zip _____

Hearts 'N Tummies Cookbook Co.
3544 Blakslee St.
Wever IA   52658
1-800-571-2665